Sexual Assault
Awareness, Prevention, Defense, Response, and Recovery

By Daniel E. Loeb, M.A.

Sexual Assault: Awareness, Prevention, Defense, Response, and Recovery

By Daniel E. Loeb

ISBN: 9798684287329

TABLE OF CONTENTS

– Introduction –

The image on the cover of this book is of the Eight of Swords Tarot card taken from the Rider-Waite-Smith deck. It shows a bound and blindfolded female, who feels all alone and surrounded by danger. The image expresses the loneliness, helplessness, despair, and vulnerability that victims of sexual assault may experience as they deal with Post-Traumatic Stress Disorder (PTSD) and begin their recovery. The author of this book spent ten years supporting victims as a Sexual Assault Prevention and Response Victim's Advocate, and an equal amount of time as a Law Enforcement Officer, investigating offenders and trying to bring them to justice. This book is the results of his experiences, and consists of the topics and concepts he wished he could have provided every victim of sexual assault before it happened, and/or to assist them in reclaiming their lives as a survivor.

In the appendix of this book there is a section containing offender profiles, but those are just general categories the FBI used to profile offenders. The truth of the matter is that rapists and sexual predators are found in every race, religion, sexual orientation, and social class. They can be anyone, and it is not necessary to understand their motives. The best anyone can do is take prudent precautions to reduce their cases of victimization, but as the tarot card on the color of this book suggests, victims and circumstances are random, and you can take every precaution and still fall victim to a predatory.

It would be nice if it were possible to determine the trustworthiness of a person by their appearance, but unfortunately, the world is much more complicated than that. In the real world, bad guys look the same as anyone else. Bad guys can't be identified by their appearance, or even by the majority of their actions. The true evildoers will behave in a manner that cloaks their intentions, and by the time they reveal their plans, it might be too late.

The bad guys are dark shadowy figures who jump out of the bushes; they look just like anyone else. They look like your teacher, your relatives, your Boy Scout leader, your priest or youth minister, your prom date, co-workers, soccer coach, or your friends. They might be that friendly frat boy who invites you to a party at his fraternity, or that helpful neighbor who offers to help you carry your groceries in, or even that relative or family friend who is known for being '*great with kids*' and keeps offering to babysit for you, so that you can have a break or enjoy a night on the town. Evildoers/bad guys/predators can be anyone. You are far more likely to be victimized by a Rapist or Child Molester that you know, than you are by a stranger.

This book will cover the following topics: Awareness, Prevention, Defense, Response, and Recovery from Rape, Sexual Assault, and/or Child Sexual Abuse. These topics are unpleasant to think about, but regrettably, the dangers they represent, and the impact/devastation caused in the lives of the victims of these crimes, necessitates the urgent need to discuss these topics, and to seriously contemplate the information.

The information contained in this book is intended for mature audiences, but parents should discuss the information they deem appropriate with their children, based on their child/teenager's individual maturity level. This book is not targeted towards children; however, children, teenagers, and young adults are especially vulnerable to rape and/or child sexual abuse, and they represent the primary age groups of the victims of these crimes.

These topics are important to discuss, because 1 in 4 women and 1 in 11 men are already victims, or will become victims of rape or sexual assault at some point in their lifetimes. If you are lucky enough not to be a victim, then there is a good chance that you know someone who is a survivor. Some of the information contained in this book may be useful to you, should you or someone close to you be sexually assaulted, or better yet, it may help you avoid becoming a victim.

Some of this information may assist you in reporting or working with the police to prosecute a crime – so that others will not suffer a similar attack from the same offender. Maybe some of this information will aid in a survivor's recovery, or encourage them to get the help they may have delayed or avoided seeking previously. Nothing in this book should be interpreted as providing any legal or psychological advice. I do not claim to be an expert, but through my experiences and education, I have acquired a wealth of information that I would like to share with others. My hope is that I can expand people's awareness of sexual assaults, prevent them from falling victim to attackers, provide them with self-defense tools (should they choose to use them), assist them in understanding the response process, and/or to provide them with information as to the aftermath and recovery some of you reading this book might one day face, or may already be experiencing.

– Chapter One –

AWARENESS

This chapter will examine some myths commonly associated with Sexual Assault, and will provide relevant definitions and statistics. Although new studies are constantly being conducted, the information and statistics regarding rape and sexual assault have not changed significantly over the past decades. Changing society's misconceptions about Sexual Assault, and more importantly, the ongoing culture of rape and sexual harassment is a very slow process. Until society changes its morals and behaviors, learning about the dangers of Sexual Assault and taking precautions to avoid becoming a victim is beneficial. The information contained in this chapter may become dated, but it will give you a general idea of what has been taking place in our country.

According to the Department of Justice's 2009 Crime Clock

- A rape occurs every two minutes.
- Every 40 seconds someone is assaulted with a deadly weapon.
- A home is burglarized every 18 seconds
- An act of domestic violence occurs each minute.
- A child is abused and/or neglected every 35 seconds
- Someone is murdered every 31 minutes.

In America, a Sexual Assault occurs every two minutes. Eighty to ninety percent of rapes go unreported. One in four Women and one in every eleven men will be Sexually Assaulted at some point during their lifetimes. 80% of Sexual Assault victims know their attacker(s). In one out of every seven sexual assault cases reported to law enforcement agencies the victims are under the age of six. Convicted rapists reported that 2/3 of their victims were under the age of 18, and 58 percent of those were under 12. 90% of the rapes of children under 12 the child knew the offender (1).

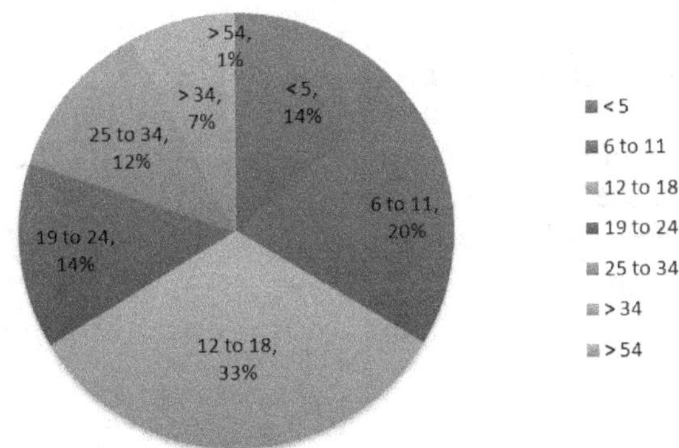

The National Center for Juvenile Justice (NCJJ, 2000), analyzed sexual assault data collected by law enforcement agencies over a five-year period; the following statistics were found to be significant among victims of sexual assault.

The study reported that 2/3 of the victims were juveniles: the 12-18 age group accounted for 33% of the victims, 20% of the victims were between six and eleven years old, children less than five years old made up 14% of the victims, Eighteen to twenty-four years old also accounted for 14% of the victims. Twenty-five to thirty-four year olds made up 12%, and over thirty-four made up 7%. Only 1% of the victims were over the age of fifty-four.

In a 2009 study, the Kansas Bureau of Investigations reported that 80.12% of rapes occurred in a residence. Of the rape assessed in that report, the weapons utilized in 77% of the rapes were 'Personal Weapons', such as the hands, feet, or body weight. No weapons were used in 14% of the rapes, and other weapons, such as knives, clubs, etc... were used in 6% of the attacks. Firearms were used in 2%.

Abducted Children

44% of abducted children are killed with the 1st hour
74% are killed within 3 hours
91% are killed within 24 hours
99% are killed within 7 days
Abductions are usually short-term and involve Sexual Assault.

Sexual Assault Defined

Sexual assault is any type of sexual activity that you do not consent to, and may include: Vaginal, anal, or oral penetration, or inappropriate touching. Rape and/or child molestation can also be defined as Sexual Assault. Each State may define the various sexual offenses differently.

U.S. Air Force Instruction 36-6001 defines Sexual Assault as, *"intentional sexual contact, characterized by use of force, threats, intimidation, abuse of authority, or when the victim does not or cannot consent. Sexual assault includes rape, forcible sodomy (oral or anal sex), and other unwanted sexual contact that is aggravated, abusive, or wrongful (to include unwanted and inappropriate sexual contact), or attempts to commit these acts."* (AFI 36-6001)

In December of 2011, FBI Director Robert S. Mueller, III, approved revisions to the Uniform Crime Reporting (UCR) Program's 80-year-old definition of rape. As approved, the UCR Program's definition of rape is, *"Penetration, no matter how slight, of the vagina or anus with any body part or object, or oral penetration by a sex organ of another person, without the consent of the victim."*

Title 10 of the U.S. Code, Subtitle A, Part II, Chapter 47, Subchapter X, Section 920, Article 120 defines Rape/Sexual Assault as:

(a) Rape: Any person subject to this chapter who commits a sexual act upon another person by—

> **(1)** using unlawful force against that other person;
> **(2)** using force causing or likely to cause death or grievous bodily harm to any person;
> **(3)** threatening or placing that other person in fear that any person will be subjected to death, grievous bodily harm, or kidnapping;
> **(4)** first rendering that other person

unconscious; or

(5) administering to that other person by force or threat of force, or without the knowledge or consent of that person, a drug, intoxicant, or other similar substance and thereby substantially impairing the ability of that other person to appraise or control conduct;

is guilty of rape and shall be punished as a court-martial may direct.

(b) Sexual Assault: Any person subject to this chapter who—

(1) commits a sexual act upon another person by—

(A) threatening or placing that other person in fear;

(B) causing bodily harm to that other person;

(C) making a fraudulent representation that the sexual act serves a professional purpose; or

(D) inducing a belief by any artifice, pretense, or concealment that the person is another person;

(2) commits a sexual act upon another person when the person knows or reasonably should know that the other person is asleep, unconscious, or otherwise unaware that the sexual act is occurring; or

(3) commits a sexual act upon another person when the other person is incapable of consenting to the sexual act due to—

(A) impairment by any drug, intoxicant, or other similar substance, and that condition is known or reasonably should be known by the person; or

(B) a mental disease or defect, or physical disability, and that condition is known or reasonably should be known by the person;

is guilty of sexual assault and shall be punished as a court-martial may direct.

Kansas Statues Annotated 21-3502 defines Rape as:

(1) Sexual intercourse with a person who does not consent to the sexual intercourse, under any of the following circumstances:

(A)   When the victim is overcome by force or fear;

(B)   When the victim is unconscious or physically powerless; or

(C)   When the victim is incapable of giving consent because of mental deficiency or disease, or when the victim is incapable of giving consent because of the effect of any alcoholic liquor, narcotic, drug or other substance, which condition was known by the offender or was reasonably apparent to the offender;

(2)   Sexual intercourse with a child who is under 14 years of age;

Sexual Assault Myths

In order to reduce the widespread occurrences of rape, we must educate society, and remove the popular myths about sexual assault. Rape myths influence perpetrators, victims, and the attitudes of the general public. Rapists and Child Molesters rely on some of these myths to either excuse their crimes, or to justify their actions to themselves. It is because of Rape Myths that juries will often contemplate the victim's attire, past sexual history, or other irrelevant information during a rape trial (that would never be considered in other criminal cases).

Cognitive Dissonance plays a vital role in the perpetrators' ability to justify his actions to himself. **Cognitive Dissonance** is the feeling of uncomfortable tension associated with holding two conflicting thoughts in the mind at the same time. Dissonance increases with a person's inability to rationalize or explain away conflicting behavior.

When a person believes something about themselves, but acts contrary to their own belief system – regarding what they consider acceptable behavior – they will seek to justify their actions to themselves in order to remove the conflict in their minds, and to justify their inappropriate behavior. If a person believes stealing is wrong, but then steals something, the person will rational an excuse for his/her behavior in order to remove the resulting conflict of emotions.

The result of Cognitive Dissonance is a change in the person's belief system; so that the person no longer believes stealing (or whatever the conflict was) is wrong in certain situations. The person modifies his/her belief system in order to accommodate his/her newly accepted belief. Once the person succeeds in excusing his/her behavior, future acts can be repeated without disturbing the person's conscience.

A rapist or child molester might utilize

existing Rape Myths to rationalize his behavior – by casting the blame on the victim i.e. *"She really wanted it"* or *"If she didn't want it, she wouldn't have...."* After justifying the behavior to themselves, perpetrators can continue repeating the behavior indefinitely without any resulting guilt.

Myth: Rape is motivated by an uncontrollable sex drive, i.e. men reach a point during sexual arousal were it becomes too late to stop (making it the woman's responsibility to end foreplay at a certain point)

Truth: Power, Control, and Entitlement are often the real motivations for rape.

Other Facts: Most sex offenders have access to consensual sex. During a Sexual Assault, <u>Rape is the Weapon, not the motive</u>. Most rapes are not impulsive acts, but are preplanned and premeditated attacks. The victim did not do anything to cause the rape; the rapist most likely set up the circumstances and environment so that the rape could occur. A study by Menachem Amir (1971) found that 71% of rapes are premeditated, and that 60% of the offenders were married and had access to consensual sex while assaulting other women. The myth that the rapist is carried away by uncontrollable sex drive, or that his behavior is a natural masculine trait, only serves as a justification for rapists – who want it to appear as though the circumstances were out of their control.

Myth: Victims invite rape (*they were asking for it*) with their appearance or behavior.

Truth: 60-70 % of rapes are preplanned by the rapist. Clothing, the time of day, the amount of alcohol in the victim's system, or any other factor/behavior is not the cause of a sexual assault. Predators look for vulnerabilities, and not attractiveness or seductive attire.

Other Facts: Bad judgment is not a rape-able offense. <u>Sexual Assault is never the victim's fault</u>; though a victim's behavior may increase her/his vulnerability to crime, bad judgment is not a justification for rape. People have a right to feel safe in their own bodies, and there isn't any activity or behavior that voids those rights. Victims often feel guilty and/or are reluctant to report a rape, because they feel that their actions (such as drinking heavily or accompanying an offender to an isolated location) may be interpreted by themselves or others as *'bringing it upon themselves'*, such attitudes are inaccurate and only perpetuate occurrences of rape within our society.

Myth: Rape only happens to "those" people.

Truth: Rape, Sexual Assault, and Child Molestation occurs within every class and within every race of people.

Other Facts: the majority of Sexual Assault victims know their attacker(s). They are boyfriends, parents, relatives, trusted family friends, youth pastors, sports coaches, etc…One concept that perpetuates rape myths is the Just World Theory.

The Just World Theory describes the tendency of people to believe that a victim's misfortune was somehow deserved. The need to view victims as receiving their just deserves is explained by psychologists as the **Just World Hypothesis**. People have a desire/need to believe that the world is an orderly, predictable, and fair place.

When tragedies occur, people tend to rationalize the horrible events claiming that the event must have somehow been the victim's fault, or that the victim must have done something to deserve it. This is a form of Cognitive Dissonance, where the people buying into the Just World Hypothesis protect themselves from the thought that they too could become the victim of a similar tragedy, by rationalizing the thought that bad things only happen to bad people.

Myth: Women make false reports of rape in order to get revenge or to otherwise protect their reputations.

Truth: Rape is one of the MOST under-reported crimes, and the least reported falsely.

Other Facts: the fact that a jury doesn't convict (due to a lack of evidence for example) or that a prosecutor permits a rapist to plea-bargain for a lesser offense, does not amount to a false report. Only around 2-5% of rape reports turn out to be false reports.

People do make false police reports, but when these do occur, it is usually done in order to commit insurance fraud or to cover up another crime. False reports of rape are extremely rare. Women do not protect their reputations by exposing their entire sexual history to several strangers within the legal process.

With the amount of Rape Myths prevalent within society – where the victim is often the one blamed – it is extremely unlikely that a woman would falsely report a rape in order to protect her reputation. When a woman does report a sexual assault, an arrest might never be made; the police might not be able to identify or find the suspect, or they might not be able to produce enough evidence to provide 'probable cause' to arrest the suspect. This does not mean that the police do not believe the victim, or that it was a false report; it just means that there was not enough evidence to make an arrest or prosecute the rapist.

Myth: Rapists are strangers who jump out of the bushes and attack women.

Truth: 85% of convicted sex offenders knew their victims. In 90% of rapes that occur on college campuses the victims knew the offenders prior to the assault.

Other Facts: Six out of ten rapes (reported by victims) occurred in their own homes, or in the home of a friend, relative or neighbor. In such situations, the victim is unlikely to report the incident, because she might feel that her judgment (of inviting the perpetrator into her home, or accompanying him to his) may be looked upon unfavorably by others (i.e. she brought in on herself by her behavior).

Myth: If she didn't want it, she could have stopped it

Truth: 84% of sexual assault victims reported the use of physical force against them. 11% involved the use of a weapon. The primary response to almost every sexual assault is fear of injury or death. **"Freezing"** is a well-documented psychological response to trauma. <u>A lack of resistance does not equate to consent.</u>

Other Facts: When faced with a violent situation, humans experience an adrenaline dump, and go into what is referred to as the Fight, Flight, or Freeze response. With adequate preparation a person may utilize this adrenaline response to assist in fighting back or escaping, but for the majority of unsuspecting victims, the freeze response is what occurs. Statistically, less than one percent rape victims are also killed during the assault; however, the majority of rape victims feel like they are in danger of being murdered. It's been said that, *"rape is a way for the rapist to murder you, and then make you go on living afterwards."*

Myth: Rape is a crime of passion (things just got carried away).

Truth: Rape is not about sex, it is about dominance. It is about Power and Control.

Other Facts: Rape is not the result of some misunderstanding. <u>It is not done by accident;</u> rapists plan their attacks in advance, and facilitate the assault by interacting with the victim, providing the victim with drugs/alcohol, or ignoring them when they say "no" and do not give clear consent. Rapists target their victims, and/or isolate them in order for the assault to take place. All of the events leading up to a sexual assault are premeditated.

Myth: Most victims sustain serious physical injuries.

Truth: 70% of rape victims reported no physical injuries, and only 4% sustained serious physical injuries – with 24% receiving minor physical injuries.

Other Facts: It is important to note that many victims who did not receive physical injuries, did however, fear being seriously injured and/or killed during the assault. 49% of victims described fearing serious injury or death during the rape. Just because a rape victim does not have bruises all over her body, that does not mean that she wasn't raped.

Rapists, especially acquaintance rapists, will often claim that the sex was consensual, which is a lot harder to do if the victims is covered with visible physical injuries. Most rapes are preplanned, and rapists also preplan how they will respond if accused of rape (because of this they will limit the amount of visible injuries to the victim).

Although the physical injuries may or may not be serious, the psychological injuries will be profound. Rape victims' lives are shattered, and the after effects can last a lifetime. Though the victims may reduce triggers and other aftereffects through therapy, a rape can never be undone, and the person will be a *'rape survivor'* for the duration of his/her life.

Sexual Assault/Abuse victims may experience Rape Trauma Syndrome, Post Traumatic Stress Disorder, and/or Post Incest Syndrome. Even if a survivor does not seek the aid of the psychiatric community, they will undergo a long and painful recovery process. Though physical injuries may be minimized, no one survives a sexual assault unharmed.

Rapists and Child Molesters rely on their victim's silence. They groom their victims in advance, and convince them that if they told on the perpetrator that they would not be believed. Often the offender is a pillar of the community. Sometimes even the victim would believe that the offender is actually a good person except for in <u>that one area </u>that the person has a problem with.

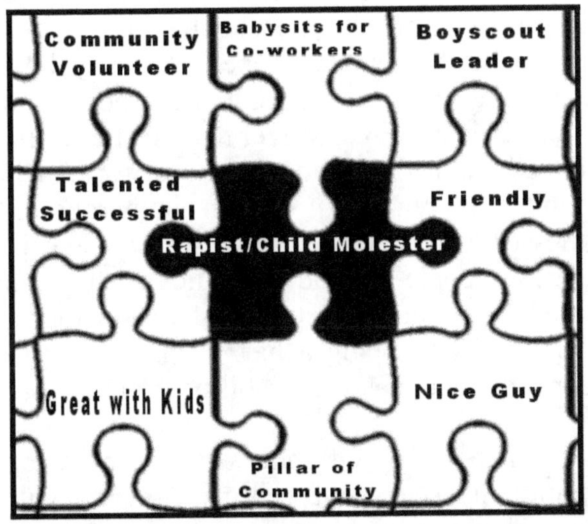

This is not true! The offender is *not* really a good person with a single dark aspect of his personality, but is a calculated predator who seeks to establish an alibi and/or establish character witnesses as part of the grooming process. They are often Pillars of the Community; they are friendly, considered great with children, nice guys, community volunteers, coaches, Boy Scout leaders, youth pastors, etc…

The truth is that these seemingly good traits are simply a disguise. The person is a wolf-in-sheep's-clothing, who establishes a false persona in order to gain access to the children, and to prepare an alibi and/or character witnesses, should the victim find the courage to report the offender.

Some of these offenders intentionally seek out troubled youth; so that if the child reports a sexual assault, the offender can rely on a wealth of character references, while the troubled youth will face bias and prejudice over his or her past behavior.

The Offender hopes to psychologically manipulate his victim during the grooming process, so that the victim would feel that he/she would not be believed if he/she did come forward, while the Offender is ready to call in numerous character witnesses who will swear that the Offender is one of the best people around – while at the same time pointing out that the victim has had a history of being a troublemaker, being a liar, drug user, or whatever other prejudice/bias/vulnerability the Offender sought out.

The Sex Offender is a predator, who intentionally seeks out victims who are vulnerable. These victims may have been attempting to escape a previous victimization situation, or they may have gotten in trouble with the law before, or may have some other situation that makes the Offender think his creditability can outweigh that of his victim – should he fail to manipulate the victim into remaining silent.

If you or someone you know has been victimized by such a person, realize, that the person was not an overall good person with a single character flaw. The person is completely evil, but seeks to establish a false persona that serves his interest by allowing him to garner people's trust, which may permit him to gain access to children or allow him to lead his intended victim to an isolated location.

A Sex Offender may have seemed nice to you, but this is only done in order to gain your trust and/or to groom you. His kindness is only an illusion; a deception that he utilizes in order to take advantage of his victims. He seeks to appear as a Pillar of the Community or as a Good Samaritan, because he wants to establish an alibi in case he needs to defend himself against accusations of his victims.

Rape is one of the most vile and evil atrocities that can be committed against another human being. It is an act that violates not only the victim's body, but also the person's ability to feel safe within her own skin.

Rape is not accomplished with a quick pull of the trigger; it is a sustained attack against someone who is in great fear/despair, and who is likely begging and pleading for mercy. Far beyond simple torture, the rapist not only enjoys hurting his victim, but he also receives sexual gratification from the abuse. Rapists and child molesters have no regard for the fear, pain, or the insurmountable psychological damage they inflict on their victims.

Rape may consist of a sudden violent attack; where a stranger pounces from a hidden location, invades a home, or abducts and takes the victim to a secondary location, but stranger rape is the less prevalent form of sexual assault.

Approximately 2/3 of rapes are committed by someone the victim knows. Of the 73% of rapes committed by non-strangers, 38% are committed by friends or acquaintances, 28% by an intimate, and 7% by relatives. Unlike popular myths about rape, the rapist is unlikely to be hiding in the bushes.

4 out of 10 rapes take place at the victim's home. 2 out of every 10 rapes take place at a friend, neighbor, or relative's home, and 1 in 12 take place in a parking garage. When a victim is assaulted at a location where she would normally feel safe; the psychological trauma is compounded, so that previous safe havens – such as the victim's own home or bedroom – no longer provides a sense of comfort or security, and the victim no longer feels safe in her own home, room, or within her own body.

Very few people have a problem believing that a stranger could commit an act of such heinous cruelty, but people are reluctant to believe a victim when the attacker is a mutual friend, co-worker, or fellow family member. Mothers may elect to side with their new husbands instead of believing their child's accusations against a stepfather, and parents may not be willing to accept the fact that their son could be a sex offender.

Due to a fear that they would not be believed (or due to fear, shame, threats, or not wanting to cause turbulence in the family), 60% of rapes go unreported. Males are even less likely to report being raped – due to feelings of being emasculated – but 10% of all rape victims are male. That number goes up drastically when dealing with children.

Child molesters are more concerned with their ability and opportunity to molest, than they are over the gender of their victims. The physical stature of men may decrease the likelihood of them being overwhelmed with force, but their physical strength does little to defend them against being drugged.

Rapists select their victims based on opportunity; it isn't what the person was wearing or doing that caused them to be targeted; it was the rapist's belief that he could victimize the person successfully. Rapists and Child Molesters are only limited by what they think they can get away with.

– Chapter Two –

PREVENTION

Rape is a violent crime, and like other violent crimes, there is no 100% guaranteed way to avoid becoming a victim. However, with adequate understanding and precautions, you can decrease your vulnerability to becoming a victim, by becoming a hard target.

In a security setting, target hardening refers to making a target more difficult or less vulnerable to attack; this is done in an effort to deter a predator, and to force them to increase the level of personal risk required to attack a target. This may cause them to select a different target that is more vulnerable. Through target-hardening, you may not be able to prevent a perpetrator from attacking someone, but you may be able to cause them to select a different victim than yourself.

In the wild, a predator is more likely to select a soft target (such as a sheep) over a hard target (such as a lion), because the predator wants to achieve its objective while exposing itself to the least amount of personal risk. Perpetrators want to successfully get away with their crimes; they don't want to get arrested, and they don't want to lose their lives. The more difficult a target is to attack, the less vulnerable it is to being attacked.

Unfortunately, evil exists in the world, and removing a perpetrator's desire or intention to commit an evil action is not possible. However, through target-hardening, we can reduce the vulnerability of a certain target by making it more difficult to attack.

Crime Triangle
Desire

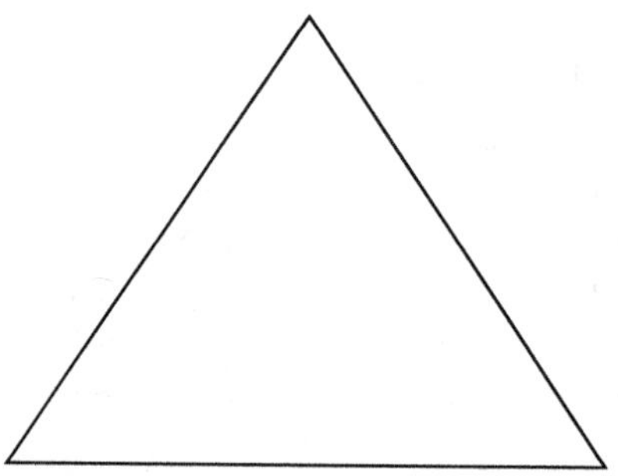

In order for a crime to take place, criminals must have a Desire to commit the crime, the Ability or Capability to do so, and an Opportunity to exploit. Removing one or more of these elements may decrease the likelihood of a crime occurring, or it may force the criminal to select an different target that offers a better likelihood of success.

You may not be able to remove a perpetrator's *Desire* to commit a crime, but you may be able to convince them to select an easier victim than yourself. Conducting yourself with confidence will act as a deterrent against many predators. In the book, *'Protecting the Gift'*, Gavin De Becker characterizes predators as being either violent predators or persuasion predators.

Violent predators initiate an attack with violence – such as ambushing their victims – but persuasion predators seek to manipulate their victims; in order to increase the person's vulnerability prior to launching an attack. Both types of predators will eventually use violence (or fear) to achieve their objectives, but the persuasion predator will first seek to lower its victim's defenses and place its victim into a position of disadvantage before initiating an attack – usually by seeking to isolate the victim or lower the victim's defenses.

Persuasion predators approach their victims in an innocent manner, and will seem friendly. Gavin De Becker describes this type of predator as a shark circling its prey. Persuasion predators do not immediately go in for the kill, but they test the waters first, in order to determine their likelihood of success. They approach their victims in a friendly manner and try to win their victim's trust and confidence.

They look for weaknesses, and wish to trick their victims into lowering their defenses in order to get them into a more vulnerable position before they attack. A persuasion predator may approach its victim using some kind of innocent ruse, so that if they are rejected, they can withdraw from that victim without creating too much suspicion.

This is similar to the lures employed by Child Molesters. The perpetrator will attempt to mask his true intentions, until he is confident that he can attack successfully. This might involve a simple ruse to trick the victim into getting into a car or into going with the perpetrator to an isolated location, or it might involve weeks or months of grooming – as certain child molesters do.

Becker states that this kind of predator will often be deterred by a little assertiveness. If someone offers you their assistance, make it clear to them that you do not need or that you do not want their help. In the use of Force Continuum, the first level of resistance that might be encountered is called, Verbal Noncompliance.

In a law enforcement setting, verbal noncompliance occurs when a suspect ignores the officer's commands – such as an instruction to drop their weapon or remain in their vehicle. When a suspect refuses to comply with a Law Enforcement Officer's commands, that is an indication that the suspect is resistant, and that an increased amount of force may be required in order to gain control of the situation.

From a victim's standpoint, verbal noncompliance could be accomplished by refusing to talk to a stranger. A persuasion predator will be unable to manipulate you into placing yourself into a position of disadvantage or isolation if you refuse to even talk to them. This level of resistance might be all that is necessary to cause a predator to look for an easier target.

Becker asserts that in today's society, people will often do things counterproductive to their own safety in order to not be perceived by a perfect stranger as being rude. The persuasion predator seeks out victims that have difficulty saying no, because by the time such a victim reaches a point when they recognize that they need to draw a line, it will usually be too late for them to do so.

Persuasion predators may initially approach their victims and ask for directions or they may offer their assistance to their would-be victims. In such situations, the predator is seeking to establish a false sense of rapport in order to gain their victim's trust and compliance; hoping to eventually get their victim into a position of disadvantage where the person can be attacked. At this point, the predator is testing the waters to gauge the intended victim's level of resistance. If the would-be victim comes across as being resistant at this point, the predator will back off and look for an easier target.

If you have children, it is important for you to teach them about persuasion predators. Pedophiles are persuasion predators and they will initiate contact with a ruse or lure, such as asking the child to assist them in locating a lost pet, or they might ask them for directions to locations the child will likely know – such as how to get to a nearby fast food restaurant – or some other ruse.

These ruses are referred to a lures, and child molesters share their tricks-of-the-trade with one another through their underground networks. Child Molesters are very organized; they have their own associations and they are constantly sharing their lures and tactics, and modifying their procedures for sharing child pornography in order to circumvent law enforcement's efforts to protect children from them.

It is important that children understand that an <u>adult will never need the assistance of a child</u>. If an adult is asking a child for assistance, then there is something wrong. If a persuasion predator initiates contact, <u>assertiveness may be all that is required to convince them to target someone else</u>. Simply stating, *"I cannot help you"* and walking away without engaging in any further dialog may be all that is needed to save you or your child's life from such a predator. To aid in the avoidance of persuasion predators, Gavin De Becker came up with seven Survival Signals, which if identified, should raise your suspicion about a person.

Becker's Survival Signals:
Force Teaming
Charm and Niceness
Too Many Details
Typecasting
Loan-sharking
The Unsolicited Promise
Discounting the Word "No"

'Force Teaming' is accomplished by the perpetrator using the word "We" or "Us" in an effort to establish a false connection, as if the two of you are in the same situation or are on the same team. Statements like, "Well, it looks like WE are going to have to wait for the next bus" or "this kind of thing always happens to people like US" or something similar, is an effort to establish a connection or build a false sense of rapport in order to gain the intended victim's trust. The perpetrator wants to make you think that they are just like you, when they aren't; you may simply be experiencing the same delay for a bus (in this example), which doesn't mean the stranger is anything like you, and simply being in the same situation, is NOT a reason to TRUST a complete stranger.

Charm and Niceness: being friendly and nice is an effort to make let your guard down. In this approach, the perpetrator is trying to charm you. They are being friendly, because they want something from you. You should be cautious of the intentions of anyone who is <u>overly friendly</u>. If your car is broken down and all of the other cars are ignoring you and driving by, yet, one person seems overly intent on helping you out, you should question the person's motives.

Going out of a person's way to assist a complete stranger is not a common trait among humans. Certainly, there are Good Samaritans out there, but any overt displays of kindness or unsolicited offers of assistance should cause you to question the motives of the person. There is always a motive. Even the Good Samaritan has a motive – such as wanting to feel good about themselves for complying with his religious beliefs. If someone is trying to charm you, then they are trying to get something from you.

Too many details: if a perfect stranger provides you with too many details, or if they answer your question with too much information, this might be a clue that the person is lying to you. Ruses and lures are preplanned and/or rehearsed; if someone is providing you with several details from a seemingly preplanned script, then you have reason to be suspicious.

An honest person will often limit the amount of information they give when providing a response to a question, because they only feel the need provide enough information to answer the question. Since liars are not confident that their explanation will be sufficient (because they are lying), they will often include more and more information in their responses, hoping to make their lies seem more believable. When a person seems to be giving you too much information, they may be trying to deceive you.

'**Typecasting**' is an attempt by the perpetrator to label or stereotype their intended victim, hoping the victim will place herself in danger in order to prove the other person wrong. This is usually done by slightly insulting the intended victim, with statements such as, *"you're not one of those overly cautious people who are afraid to walk through a park at night, are you?"* Their hope being that you will reply, *"of course not"* and then place yourself into a dangerous and isolated situation simply to prove to a complete stranger that you are not scared. Don't place yourself into danger just to prove that you are not chicken.

'**Loan-sharking**' or reciprocity is an old salesmen's trick designed to make you feel obligated to the giver. This manipulation is usually accomplished by a perpetrator giving the target an inexpensive gift in order to make the person feel indebted to him. The salesman may provide a person with a cheap promotional item, hoping the target will feel obligated to buy something, or at least listen to the person's sales pitch.

Predators may exploit an offer of assistance, such as assisting a victim with carrying their groceries, in an effort to either set the person up to be attacked, or to begin a conversation that will permit the predator to use a ruse or other manipulation (i.e.

listen to their sales pitch).

Gavin De Becker states that you should always be wary of an 'Unsolicited Promise' - promises are used to help convince you of something, but they are of little value and a guarantee from a perfect stranger is worthless. If someone gives you an Unsolicited Promise, ask yourself why the person is trying to convince you of something.

The Promise is not evidence of anything; it provides no guarantee, and should have no value other than to cause you to question why the person is trying to convince you to trust them without cause.

Discounting the word "No"; if someone ignores you when you tell them "No" over a small matter, you certainly should not trust that they will respect your wishes over something more important. If someone says "No", but then allows the person to ignore their "No", then the persuasion predator may be encouraged by this response, and may continue in his manipulation.

Verbal Noncompliance is the first level of resistance; if the victim fails to resist at this level, or allows her resistance to be ignored, then the perpetrator will not be dissuaded unless confronted with a different level of resistance.

After Verbal Noncompliance, the next level of resistance requires some form of physical resistance, and by the time a person who allows her "No" to be discounted reaches the point that she decides she has no choice except to physically resist, the persuasion predator will probably have already placed his victim into a position of disadvantage.

Stranger Rape

There are three categories of Stranger Rape: the Blitz Attack, the Contact Sexual Assault, and the Home Invasion Sexual Assault.

A Blitz Attack refers to situations where the rapist rapidly and violently attacks his victims with no prior contact. These attacks usually occur at night and in a public place. This is the type of stranger attack that people most commonly associate with rape – where a stranger leaps out from behind some bushes as rapes a jogger in an isolated area. Statistically, this type of attack is the rarest.

Contact Sexual Assault – refers to situations where the rapist has prior contact with the victim, and tries to gain her trust before initiating the sexual assault. This type of rapist is a Persuasion Predator, who picks his victims a bars or other public areas and attempts to lure his victim into cars, places of isolation, or otherwise tries to coerce the victim into a situation where a sexual assault can occur.

Home Invasion Sexual Assaults are when a stranger breaks into his victim's home in order to commit the rape. This may involve breaking into the home when the victim is asleep, or the perpetrator might use a ruse in order to gain access to the victim's home; such as pretending his car has broken down and needing to use the phone, or masquerading as a serviceman needing to check the utilities.

The perpetrator might have stalked his victim by following her home previously, and gathering information regarding his victim's daily activities. The rapist could then break into the victim's home when the victim is completing a routine/daily task, and the rapist could wait for her to return.

He also might have been a serviceman (such as a plumber or other repairman) that has done work at the home, or a mailman or delivery person that allowed him to survey the place previously. To guard again Home Invasions, you should always vary your routines; practice situational awareness to determine if you are being followed, or if someone is paying undue attention to you. You should also limit access to your home by repairmen and delivery persons.

Having a dog and/or a burglar alarm, may warn you if someone tries breaking into your home when you are asleep – giving you time to lock yourself in a secure room or arm yourself – and a burglar alarm can alert you to someone breaking into your home when you are away, so that you don't come home and find someone waiting for you there.

Acquaintance Rape

Date Rape is a major form of sexual assault, but this type of sexual assault is not done by a stranger. Date rapists will employ many of the same techniques as the persuasion predator, and will manipulate their intended victims, try to isolate them, ignore the victim's "No's", and so forth, but the situation is unique, because the victims often like the perpetrator prior to the event – making the sexual assault more difficult to defend against.

A person might be able to identify warning signs from a stranger – such as attempts to isolate – but things are more complicated when dealing with a suitor; because right up until to the point that the perpetrator initiates the sexual assault, the intended victim may still be trying to avoid offending the perpetrator, and hoping the person will like them and/or get into or stay in a relationship with the suitor.

Of course, once a person is raped, she will no longer want to have anything to do with the rapist (except for in certain domestic violence situations), but prior to a rape occurring, the victim's judgment might be clouded – not wanting to believe that Mr. Right, is actually a bad guy.

Even when you like a person, and are hoping to be in or to remain in a relationship with him, you must place your safety first. The bottom line is that once a person goes too far, you need to recognize that there is no hope for a future relationship, and must look out for your own safety. If someone is trying to rape you, then they are not the person you thought they were, and he certainly is not someone you will try to continue a relationship with.

If someone discounts your objections, he does not respect you, and you need to place yourself and your safety above any hope you previously had about having a relationship with the person. Up until you are sure about your safety and the intentions of your suitor, you need to employee the same safety measures you would with strangers, such as not being isolated from friends or taken to an isolated location, not becoming overly intoxicated, or allowing him to discount your objections or to invade your boundaries.

The "I's" of Sexual Assault

When dealing with Sexual Assault prevention, the concept of the "Five I's" is one approach promoted as a means of identifying and/or avoiding danger. Sexual Assaults usually have one or more of these elements involved, and although these elements may be present in completely innocent situations, they can serve as warning signs to practice diligence and evaluate your safety.

Invasion (includes Interest or Inappropriateness)
Ignoring
Isolation
Intoxication and Instincts

Invasion: perpetrators often invade their would-be victim's personal space, either visually, verbally, and/or physically. This behavior is done to make the person uncomfortable and to test their boundaries. The behavior may seem flirtatious, but it is intended to make the victim uncomfortable.

Visually, the person might be starring, looking the victim up and down, or displaying excessive eye contact. This undue **interest** may provide a clue that the person is being targeted or sized up.

Verbally, the perpetrator might make **inappropriate** comments, ask questions that are too personal, or make dirty jokes.

Physically, the perpetrator might **invade** the victim's personal space, stand too close, or engage in inappropriate touching (such as accidentally rubbing against the victim). If someone invades your space or make you feel uncomfortable through their behavior, either visually, verbally, or physically, then these are signs to be on guard against the person.

Such behavior by itself may not indicate that you are currently in danger, but it should cause you to be suspicious of the person. If such behavior is combined with some of the other I's, such as intoxication and isolation, then the level of danger the person is in would be increased.

Ignoring: If someone ignores your verbal or non-verbal communication that is a sign that you should be suspicious of the person. Verbal Noncompliance is the first level of resistance. If you say, *"No"* and a person ignores you, the person is attempting to overcome your resistance to them, and they are actively resisting you by resisting your verbal commands. You have a right to your personal space, and people need to respect your wishes and boundaries. If someone isn't showing you respect, then you should be cautious of them.

Isolation: is a major element of sexual assaults. Be cautious of anyone who tries to isolate you; by getting you to go to an isolated location, or by getting you away from your friends or other sources of support. The need to avoid isolation cannot be overly stressed. Perpetrators want to isolate you, so that no one will hear you scream, or come to your aid, and so you can't get away. They also do not want people to witness what they do to you.

Intoxication: Perpetrators use alcohol and/or drugs to make someone more vulnerable. Drugs and alcohol are a factor in approximately 90% of sexual assaults. Rapists use drugs or alcohol to make their victims more vulnerable, or as an excuse for their own behavior. Being intoxicated makes it more difficult for victims to respond physically, and they are less mentally alert to manipulations, ruses, and attempts to isolate them or to otherwise set them up to be raped.

Being intoxicated does not cause or invite a person to be raped or sexually assaulted, but it does make a person more vulnerable to it. It might also deter a victim from coming forward, because the victim may be too embarrassed by her own behavior and/or stereotypes/myths about rape, or the victim might not want to admit to drinking underage or using illegal drugs.

Regardless of a victim's level of intoxication or actions, nothing gives a person the right to force sex on someone else. The perpetrator is always the one who is responsible for his crime, and regardless of the victim's behavior, clothing, or decisions, nothing gives a person the right to victimize others.

Instincts: in all situations, you need to trust your instincts. If something makes you feel uncomfortable or causes you to experience a sense of fear, then you probably have reason to be afraid. <u>Do not take any chances with your safety</u>. You need to consider yourself and your safety as the most important thing – offending others or coming off as being rude is acceptable.

Perpetrators rely on people ignoring their instincts, and exploit that fact in order to gain an advantage. Trust your intuition. If you feel uncomfortable in a situation, then take action to ensure your safety, such as leaving the area or regrouping with friends.

Invasion, Ignoring, Isolation, Intoxication, and

Instincts are known as the Five I's, and can serve as clues to signal you to the possibility of sexual assault. However, those five concepts are not all inclusive.

Becoming a Hard Target

Report suspicious people or situations to the police; predators will continue to assault others until law enforcement has enough legal grounds to prosecute them – if there is not enough evidence to prosecute an offender the first time, as more and more women make reports, it becomes increasingly difficult for the offender to claim there was a misunderstanding.

Remember that most rape victims are raped by someone they know, so keep your guard up, and only go out with people you know well. Meet dates in public places. Provide your own transportation so that you can leave whenever you want/need to, and so that you do not have to rely on others.

Tell someone where you are going, who you are meeting, and when you will return. Whenever possible, go out with a group of people, and don't be left alone with a suitor until you know him better. Have a cell phone with you at all times, and don't allow yourself to be isolated or taken out of cell phone range or out of public view (if you call 9-1-1, they should be able to obtain your GPS coordinates, and will be able to send you assistance even if you are not sure where you are).

Don't feel that you "owe" anybody anything. Loan-sharking and Reciprocity are common manipulative techniques; just because someone bought you dinner, gave you a gift, or did you a favor, that does not mean you owe them anything. Never compromise yourself, or allow someone to make you feel obligated to do something you do not want to do.

Don't be manipulated by lines such as, *"If you loved me, you'd..."* The fact is, if the person loved you, then he would respect your wishes and wait until you were ready. <u>Be assertive</u>; respect yourself enough to not do anything you do not want to do. <u>You matter, and deserve respect</u>.

Be extremely cautious of going into someone else's home, or even inviting someone into your home. Those are isolated locations and may be dangerous. Three out of Five Rapes occur in either the victim's home, or in the home of an acquaintance.

When going out with friends, work as a team, and look out for each other. Don't allow yourself or your friends to become isolated. Know where your friends are and leave together. If one of your friends begins acting out of character or seems overly intoxicated, get her to a safe place immediately. If you think either you or one of your friends has been drugged, call the police and or the facility's security immediately, and do not leave until someone you trust comes to pick you up.

When at home keep your doors and windows locked, and don't open the door for a stranger. Avoid walking or jogging alone, stay in well-lit and visible areas. Vary your routines and be unpredictable. Don't use headphones in both ears, which might make you less aware of your surroundings.

Maintain situational awareness, and notice if someone is paying undue attention to you. Trust your instincts, and place your safety needs ahead of appearing rude. Never hitchhike or pick up hitchhikers. Keep a cell phone with you, and maintain your vehicle so that it doesn't break down.

If your car does break down, stay in the car with the doors locked, and call the police. If you don't have a phone, place a sign in the back window of your car that says, *"Help, Call the Police."* If someone stops to help, stay in the car, and if they want to help, ask them to call the police for you. Claims that they will try to fix the car for you or offers to drive you to a gas stations could be attempts to isolate or abduct you.

Make your limits clear before getting into a sexual situation, and do not allow someone to ignore you when you tell them *"No"* or *"Stop."* If your objections are ignored, clearly state, *"This is rape!"* That statement is clear and avoids any possible misunderstandings. If a person continues to ignore your objections, then further resistance actions are warranted and may be required – such as physical resistance in order to escape.

Avoid getting overly intoxicated. If you do drink in public, get your own drinks, and/or make sure you observe it being made. Do not drink from punch bowls or drinks that have been previously mixed, and never leave your drink unattended.

Date Rape drugs are widely available, and can severely limit your ability to resist being raped. They aid the perpetrator by making it easier for him to overpower you, and can be employed against anyone. Don't let the term Date Rape fool you, drug induced rapes can occur at anytime, and can be employed by complete strangers as a means of isolating and incapacitating the victim.

The drugs are often odorless, colorless, and tasteless, and can easily be added to flavored drinks. There are several different drugs utilized in sexual assaults with various side effects – to include convulsions, hallucinations, loss of consciousness, and death. They impair the victim's mental and physical ability to protect him or herself, and may cause the person to blackout or not remember the attack the following day.

If you feel that you have been drugged and raped, get medical attention right away. Let the medical staff know about your concerns, so they can test you for the drugs, sexual transmitted diseases, and so on. Don't urinate, douche, bathe, brush your teeth, wash your hands, change clothes, or eat or drink anything before you go – so that a sexual assault forensic exam can gather evidence, and you can receive proper medical treatment.

Sometimes, despite your best efforts and application of prevention strategies, saying *"no"* might not be able stop a sexual assault. The majority of sexual assaults are planned out in advance, and the perpetrator will have directed the events in order to isolate you and to place you into a position of vulnerability and disadvantage.

There is no set of rules or specific advice that you can apply in every given situation, because every situation will be unique. Finding yourself trapped in a violent and dangerous situation may be unavoidable. However, with prior planning and forethought, you might be able avoid the freeze response, and give yourself a better opportunity to weigh your options in the heat of the moment – allowing you to avoid making a critical decision on the spot in the midst of a violent and fluid situation.

When faced with a violent situation, you should make a decision and <u>Act Immediately</u>. Trust in your intuition and escape if you can. Never give into the person's sexual advances hoping that you will be able to find a way to stop him later. You must realize that the longer you allow a situation to continue, the more dangerous it will become for you.

The perpetrator is not going to stop. The attack is most likely a preplanned assault, and the more successful the perpetrator believes himself to be, the more emboldened he will become, and the more difficult it will be for you to dissuade his advances.

Compose yourself, try to think clearly and regain control of your senses following the fear and adrenaline dump that will occur when you experience fight, flight, or freeze physiological phenomenon. <u>Passive Resistance</u>, such as attempting to talk the perpetrator out of the assault, or attempts to cause him to view you as a friend (or even as a human being) are unlikely to be successful.

The assault is most likely preplanned, and it is very likely that this is not his first time engaging in such behavior. The type of person who sets out to rape another person is evil, and unlikely to sympathize with your fear, tears, begging, crying, or pleading. Depending in the rapist's psychological profile, the rapist may even Get Off, on the fear and torment he creates in his victim.

<u>Active Resistance</u>: physically resisting (defending yourself), may be an alternative, but it must be based on the situation at hand. You might be out numbered, drugged, lack self-defense skills, or there may be some other factor that causes you to believe that resistance would be futile.

Active Resistance may provide you with a

means of escaping. Most rapists do not cause serious physical injury during their assaults, because they want to claim the sex was consensual if they are unable to scare you into not reporting the attack to the police.

The amount of physical violence a rapist intends to inflict during the rape, is part of the rapist's profile, and is unlikely to be effected by your actions – whether you chose to resist or not. If you do decide to resist and the rapists strikes you a few times in order to regain control, any bruises or damage you sustain will only add to your case, and damage the rapist's ability to claim consensual sex if you prosecute. A black eye or broken nose will heal, but such visible signs of resistance will make it very difficult for the rapist to claim the sex was consensual.

<u>Submitting</u> is always an option. You might find yourself in a situation where submitting is your only choice, or is the best choice for the situation you find yourself in. It is important for you to trust your decisions, and know that whatever decision you made in order to survive was the correct decision.

During robberies, when the criminal is only after your money (and not your person) victims are advised to submit to the robbery and hand over their belongings without a fight in order to have the ordeal end as quickly as possible. During a robbery, submitting is usually the better option, because your belongings can be replaced, you can't.

The situation is very different when the criminal is after you, and not your belongings. In such a situation, resistance might be a better option, but it will depend on the unique situation you find yourself in. You might not have a choice except to submit to being raped; if that is the case, there are still some things you can do to that might assist you later. Such as trying to obtain DNA evidence from the perpetrator, like some hair or getting some of his skin under your fingernails.

Following a non-stranger rape, the perpetrator will probably try to convince you that telling anyone about the rape would be futile. He may use rape myths or other preplanned justifications in an attempt to dissuade you from reporting the rape to the authorities. He might attempt to convince you that you really wanted it, or that because of your behavior, such as dancing with him all night, drinking, doing drugs, accompanying him to a secluded location, inviting him in, and so on, that no one would believe you if you tell on him.

Arguing with a rapist at this point would be pointless, and might serve only to prolong his attempts to convince you that the whole thing was actually your fault. Do whatever you think is best to get out of that situation, and return to a safe location. Once you are in a safe location, do not bath, douche, change clothes, brush your teeth, or do anything that might contaminate any forensic evidence that may exist on your body.

Call a sexual assault hotline and gain the assistance of a Sexual Assault Victim's Advocate, and/or a close friend or family member, and ask them to accompany you to the hospital. Once there, you will undergo a Sexual Assault Nurse's Examination (SANE), and forensic evidence will be collected, and stored, so that you will have the option of seeking criminal charges later if you chose to.

Immediately following a rape is not the time to decide whether or not you wish to prosecute. Having a SANE completed will allow you to keep that option open, should you choose to prosecute the perpetrator later. In addition to the collection of forensic evidence, you should get medically check out to ensure you do not have any physical injuries, and to receive immediate care to avoid STDs or pregnancy. More information on how to respond to a rape will be discussed in the response chapter.

The information in this section was meant to provide you with a better understanding of sexual assault and to provide some precautions you can take that may aid in the prevention of rape. Unfortunately, there is no sure way to guarantee success. You can do everything right, and still be a victim of rape. Action always beats reaction, and in the case of sexual assault, the victim is always reacting to the situation.

The majority of rapes are preplanned, and the perpetrators have the luxury of time and advance planning to orchestrate their crimes. Victims are only able to respond to the situations they find themselves in. Rapists and child molesters set their victims up, and create the ideal situation for victimization before initiating their attacks. The sad truth is that you can do everything right, and still become a victim.

If you do become a victim of rape, it is <u>imperative</u> that you to understand <u>that it was not your fault</u>. It is NEVER the victim's fault. Blame always rests 100% with the rapist. It doesn't matter how you were dressed, how much you drank, what you did, how you behaved, what you said or think you should have said; sexual assaults are NEVER the victim's fault.

There is nothing that the victim did to justify being raped. No one has the right to invade another person's boundaries. Everyone has a right to feel safe in their own bodies. It is never the victim's fault, and the blame should always be directed at the perpetrator. Sexual Offenders preplan their crimes; they coordinate with other offenders, share tactics, and manipulate and set their victims up.

Victims are only able to respond to the situations they find themselves in. The perpetrators create the situations; they circumvent their victim's defenses, find ways to isolate their victims, drug their victims, deceive their victims, coerce and overpower their victims. Some people are evil, and like all other crimes, the victims can take every precaution, do everything right, and still be victimized.

If you are a sexual assault survivor, you need to understand that it was not your fault. It had nothing to do with anything you did or didn't do. You have nothing to feel guilty or ashamed about. You were placed in a horrible situation, and if you are still here today, then whatever you did in order to survive was the correct thing do to. Do not dwell on *'what ifs'* or contemplate "*what you should have done.*"

There is no correct answer. Every situation is unique, and only the person in the situation can determine the best way to respond based on the unique circumstances and their gut instincts. Whatever you did to survive the situation was the correct decision, because you are still here.

– Chapter Three –

DEFENSE

When a predator ignores your objections or when you are being violently assaulted, you may choose to, or be left with no other choice but to physically resist. Every situation is unique, and there is no correct answer regarding how to respond to a certain situation. The decision as to whether or not to defend yourself is an individual one, and must be made in the heat of the moment, based on the totality of the circumstances you find yourself in.

The information contained in this section is not meant to provide you with a step-by-step self-defense process, but hopefully, it will provide you with some options that may assist you, if you believe they are necessary. Before we examine different methods of self-defense, it is important to understand your right to self-defense and the legal ramifications associated with it.

Different situations require different levels of force. Deadly force is not warranted in many situations, and using an inappropriate amount of force can have legal and criminal ramifications. Techniques that possess the potential of killing the opponent or inflicting great bodily injury are considered deadly force techniques, and should only be utilized if the situation warrants it.

Every person possesses the 'Inherent Right to Self Defense.' This right is not given to you by any government or law; though the principle is recognized in Federal, State, and International Laws. The

Declaration of Independence states that people were, *"endowed by their Creator with certain unalienable Rights that among these are Life, Liberty and the Pursuit of Happiness* (Declaration of Independence July 4, 1776)."

These same principles are reaffirmed in the United Nations' Universal Declaration of Human Rights, which reads, *"Everyone has the right to life, liberty and security of person."* The Declaration of Independence identifies the *'Right to Life'* as an unalienable right given to man by their Creator. The founding fathers did not give us the *'Right to Life'* when drafting the U.S. Constitution, but they did seek to protect it.

The Fourth Amendment to the U.S. Constitution stresses the right of the people to be secure in their persons. The Fifth Amendment expands on this right and ensures that no citizen will be *"deprived of life, liberty, or property, without due process of law."* The Fifth Amendment ensures that no U.S. citizen will have their life taken from them without first receiving due process.

The ideal means of dealing with criminals who seek to take away your 'Right to Life' is to have them arrested and tried for attempted murder. However, when your life is being threatened, you do not have time to appeal to the civil magistrate in the matter, and you may be left with no other choice except to defend your inherent right to life.

In his Second Treatise of Government, John Locke wrote, *"My own defense, and the right of war, a liberty to kill the aggressor, because the aggressor allows not time to appeal to our common judge, nor the decision of the law, for remedy in a case where the mischief may be irreparable... And therefore it is lawful for me to treat him as one who has put himself into a state of war with me, i.e., kill him if I can; for to that hazard does he justly expose himself, whoever introduces a state of war and is aggressor in it..*"

As Locke pointed out, when you are in a life or death situation, you are left with no choice except to defend yourself, because your only other option is to be killed. When an aggressor threatens your existence (or great bodily harm), the aggressor prevents you from using the legal system as it was intended, and leaves you with no alternative except to defend yourself.

In Graham v. Connor, 490 U.S. 386 (1989), the US Supreme Court established the fourth amendment standard of *"objective reasonableness"* as the appropriate standard for assessing the use of force in the context of making an arrest or other seizure of a person. It explained its application in these terms: *The question is whether the officers' actions are 'objectively reasonable' in light of the facts and circumstances confronting them..... The reasonableness of a particular use of force must be judged from the perspective of a reasonable officer on the scene, rather than with the 20/20 vision of hindsight. ...the 'reasonableness' inquiry...is an objective one...."*

Florida Statute 776.012 *Use of force in defense of person.--A person is justified in using force, except deadly force, against another when and to the extent that the person reasonably believes that such conduct is necessary to defend himself or herself or another against the other's imminent use of unlawful force. However, a person is justified in the use of deadly* *force and does not have a duty to retreat if: (1) He or she reasonably believes that such force is necessary to prevent imminent death or great bodily harm to himself or herself or another or to prevent the imminent commission of a forcible felony*

The Florida statute states that the citizen does not have a "Duty to Retreat." This is an important element to self-defense laws that you must check for in the statutes of the State you reside in. Some States require you to attempt to retreat before you are authorized to use force in self-defense. Kansas is another State – like Florida – that does not require a duty to retreat. Kansas Statute 21-3218 states, "*A person who is not engaged in an unlawful activity and who is attacked in a place where such person has a right to be has no duty to retreat and has the right to stand such person's ground and meet force with force.*"

In the Florida statute, deadly force is also authorized to prevent a forcible felony. The State of Florida defines a Forcible Felony as, "*treason; murder; manslaughter; sexual battery; carjacking; home-invasion robbery; robbery; burglary; arson; kidnapping; aggravated assault; aggravated battery; aggravated stalking; aircraft piracy; unlawful throwing, placing, or discharging of a destructive device or bomb; and any other felony which involves the use or threat of physical force or violence against any individual.*" Any citizen of Florida is authorized to use deadly force in order to prevent the imminent commission of the above felony crimes.

Sexual Battery is listed as one of the forcible felonies in the Florida Statute that deadly force is authorized in. However, it is important to note, that minus the forcibly felony statement, deadly force is authorized when a person reasonably believes it is necessary in order to prevent imminent death or great bodily harm. Although only a small percentage of rape victims are also murdered, rape victims often experience enormous fear and believe they are in imminent danger of death. It's been said that rape is a way for the rapist to murder his victim, but then force her to go on living afterwards. Regardless of the presence of the forcibly felony terminology, it is objectively reasonable for a rape victim to believe she is in imminent danger of death or serious bodily harm when being assaulted. So in response to an attempted rape, a victim responding with deadly force would in most circumstances be reasonable.

Florida 776.013 Home protection; use of deadly force; presumption of fear of death or great bodily harm.-- (1) A person is presumed to have held a reasonable fear of imminent peril of death or great bodily harm to himself or herself or another when using defensive force that is intended or likely to cause death or great bodily harm to another if: (a) The person against whom the defensive force was used was in the process of unlawfully and forcefully entering, or had unlawfully and forcibly entered, a dwelling, residence, or occupied vehicle, or if that person had removed or was attempting to remove another against that person's will from the dwelling, residence, or occupied vehicle

The Florida statute states that the mere fact that someone broke in to a home or occupied vehicle is enough to establish the reasonable fear of death or great bodily injury, so the objectively reasonable standard is automatically met.

ESCALATION OF FORCE	
Subjects Actions	**Appropriate Response**
Compliant	Verbal Commands
Resistant (Passive)	Contact Techniques
Resistant (Active)	Control Techniques (Come-Alongs)
Assaultive (Bodily Harm)	Defensive Tactics (Punches/Kicks)
Assaultive (Death/Great Bodily Harm)	Deadly Force

Escalations of Force Models (also referred to as Use of Force Continuums) are used by law enforcement personnel in order to tailor their response to the actions of a suspect. The basic principle of the model is to, *"use only that force reasonably necessary to reach your objective."* Once a level of force is no longer required, you must discontinue its use and apply a more appropriate level of force. For example, if a suspect reaches the Assaultive (Bodily Harm) phase of the model and is subsequently subdued – using the appropriate amount of force – once handcuffed, striking the suspect with a baton in order to gain further compliance would be considered excessive force.

Use of force models are basically a way of applying the appropriate degree of force to the given situation. These same principles are expected during civilian self-defense situations, but civilians are unlikely to have all of the same types of force available to them that law enforcement officers do. The degrees of force used by civilians are either the lawful use of force or the use of deadly force (based on the situation).

An important concept to understand while dealing with Use of Force issues is that you are dealing with types and levels of force. You are matching the level of force to the level of force being confronted. Minimum Force does not mean that if confronted by a knife wielding predator that you must attempt to use pain compliance techniques or non-lethal weapons. If someone is wielding a knife then you are being confronted with deadly force, and you can respond with deadly force.

Matching force for force also does not mean that you have to use the same weapon as your opponent; if your opponent has a knife and you have a gun, both weapons are capable of applying deadly force – you do not need to have the exact same weapon in order to apply a proportional amount of force.

When dealing with Use of Force issues, law enforcement agencies, military organizations, States, and Countries all have slightly different rules, statutes, and laws in place, but everyone has an inherent right to self-defense. This right was not given to you by any government or law; you inherited the right to life by being born. Your Inherent Right to Self-Defense is a byproduct of your Unalienable Right to Life, which was endowed to you by your Creator, is protected by the Constitution of the United States, and by State and International Laws.

The only requirement for self-defense is that your actions be <u>reasonable</u> based upon your perception of the situation you are in. However, since some States may require a duty to retreat before using force in self-defense, it is important that you research the applicable laws in the State or Country you reside in.

In response to an attempted Rape, you are left with very few options. You can fight back, try to escape, or give in. When faced with such a horrifying situation, your body will go into its Fight, Flight, or Freeze response, and those will pretty much be the options you have to choose from. When you are being victimized by a violent offender, it is important to realize that the person is not like you. Just because you might show mercy or listen to reason, that does not mean that your attacker will. The attack is most likely premeditated, and it is probably not the first time your attacker has done this. He is not going to sympathize with you, listen to reason, show pity or mercy, or be talked out of it.

If you do choose to resist, your objective should be to escape – fight back in order to get an opportunity to escape. If you have been targeted, the perpetrator probably selected you as a victim, because he believes he can be successful in his crime. He thinks he is able to overpower you. He may be bigger and stronger than you, or threaten you with a weapon; in any case, at least in your attacker's perception, he does not view you as someone who is going to be able to beat him in a fight. Unless you actively and routinely practice your fighting abilities through boxing or martial arts, your chances of beating up the attacker are very limited. Your objective should be to fight back until you are able to escape. If you get the opportunity to escape, take it, don't attempt to subdue the attacker and hold him for the police.

When deciding whether or not to resist, some people worry that resisting might only make matters worse. In his book, *'Strong on Defense: Survival*

Rules to protect you and Your Family from Crime' Sanford Strong wrote that *'Doing Nothing'* is the biggest risk of all. If you choose to do nothing, or remain frozen with fear, your chances of escaping later become more difficult, and the likelihood of violence may escalate. To contrast the choices of *'Doing Something'* (Resisting) verses *'Doing Nothing'* (Submitting), Strong referred to a Department of Justice Study on Rape that was published in 1985. He noted the following facts about rape:

- Unlike armed robbers and home intruders, rapists do not normally prearm themselves with weapons. Only 23 percent of 1.6 million cases studied involved men armed with knives or guns, with an equal break of 11 percent knives, 12 percent guns. The major exception to this were rapists who break into a residence; 96 percent grab a knife from the kitchen.

- Approximately 51 percent of women resisted in some form, ranging from screaming to fleeing, to fighting back; the remaining 49 percent did nothing.

- Over 96 percent of all the injuries for both women who resisted or did not were abrasions, lacerations; yet, this statistic was not affected by the rapist's wielding a weapon or determined by the victim's resistance, as old myths once declared. When broken down between resistance or submission, there was only an increase of 2 percent in the injury level to the women who resisted.

- Under 4 percent received major injuries that

required a prolonged hospital stay; and the majority of those were raped in an isolated area or trapped in a home or apartment. Gang rape, protracted torture by one or more foreign objects, all require time while isolated and controlled.

- Only .03 percent were also murdered, the lowest percentage of all violent crimes.

No one can tell you how to respond in a certain situation, because every violent encounter is unique. You will feel like your life is in danger – or even that you are being murdered – but statistically you have a good chance of surviving the situation, and resisting may also prevent you from being raped, which could save you enormous emotional turmoil. You may be injured while resisting, but the injuries you sustain may seem small in comparison to the life shattering effect a completed rape might have on you. Injuries may also aid in corroborating your account of the events, which may assist in the prosecution of the rapist.

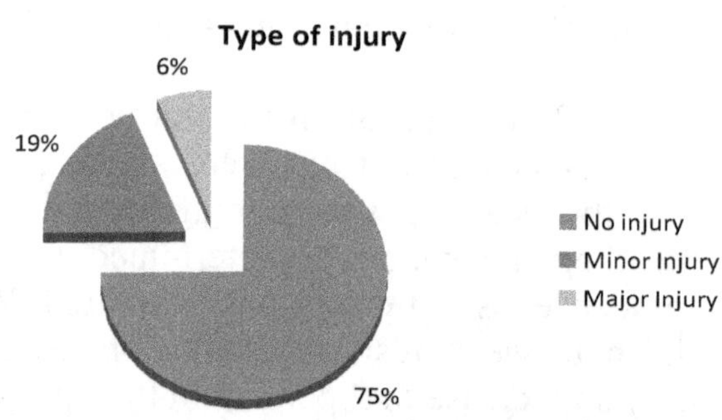

(Injuries in Kansas 2009)

Of the rape related injuries documented in

Kansas in 2009, only 6% of victims received major injuries. 19% of the victims received minor injuries, and the majority, 75% of the victims received no physical injuries. The 1985 Department of Justice study reported that those who resisted only increased their percentage of injury by 2%, which is a fair tradeoff, considering that it might afford them the opportunity to escape and spare them from the profound psychological injury of being raped. Also, any bruises or injuries sustained may assist the victim later, should she choose to press charges against the offender. A black eye or broken nose will heal, but such visible injuries will go a long way in preventing the offender from convincing a jury that the sex was consensual.

When faced with a violent situation, humans experience an adrenaline dump, and their bodies go into what is referred to as the Fight, Flight, or Freeze response. They experience an adrenal dump, which distorts their perception. They may experience tunnel vision, auditory exclusion, the world may seem to be moving in slow motion, or extremely fast.

Blood is shifted from the extremities back to the central core. This is done to strengthen the life supporting organs, so blood is available to the brain and so they will not bleed out as fast if injured. The body is prepared to fight (defend itself), or flight (to make a run for it), but if a person is not expecting these physiological changes, their response might be to freeze.

The freeze response occurs because the blood has shifted for the legs and arms back to the central core, the body does this to reinforce the life supporting organs, but the limited amount of blood in the extremities may make it difficult to move those body parts. This is compounded by the adrenal dump and chemical changes that distort the person's mental faculties, so that if a person isn't prepared for these changes, instead of being more capable of fighting or fleeing, the person may not be able to move, or think of what to do. So instead of taking action, they stand there motionless, frozen with fear, like a deer in headlights.

In the book, '*Raising Kids Who can Protect themselves*' Debbie Gardner suggests BST as a means for children to overcome the freeze response, and to enable them to regain the functionality required to escape. BST stands for Breath, Space, and Throat. Gardner reports that during the freeze response the scared person holds his or her breath and the body shuts down. Since the blood leaves the arms and legs and goes to the central core, the petrified person is unable to move, and without breathing, they are unable to scream or call for help.

To remedy this, Gardner suggests the child make a fist – coupled with taking a deep breath – which forces blood back into the arms, allowing the child to regain his or her ability to move. Taking a deep breath also allows the child to speak and yell for help. The S in Gardner's BST stands for Space, as a reminder for the child to protect his/her boundaries (personal space). The T stands for Throat, which is the target of the child's attack, when his/her boundaries are threatened. The book also encourages the child to roar and categorizes words into different colors; teaching the child that sometimes it is appropriate to use foul language, in order to distract or deter a predator.

A persuasion predator may expect a child to

respond in a polite manner, which the perpetrator is ready to manipulate and counter the child's response. A child's polite statement such as, *"I'm sorry sir, I not supposed to talk to strangers"* might be met with the perpetrator's pre-rehearsed response outlining why it is okay to talk to a stranger in this situation. However, when a child takes a deep breath, balls her fists, takes a step back, and roars, *"Get the fuck away from me!"* the persuasion predator is met with verbal resistance that he is probably not expecting.

When backed into a corner, even an otherwise harmless pussycat can appear menacing – a predator may be much bigger and believe it can subdue the cat, but if the predator thinks it might get scratched, it may decide to alter its plans. If the persuasion predator is not yet committed to launching his attack, he might disengage and look for an easier target.

To link the roar principle to Gardner's BST acronym, I add an E for *'Exclaim'*, making BST, BEST. These principles do not need to occur in a specific order; children and adults can remember that when confronted with danger (and upon noticing themselves experiencing a freeze response), they can Breath while making a fist to get the blood moving, Exclaim or yell, to get the attention of bystanders and/or to deter or distract the predator, Space, to remember to guard their boundaries, and Throat, to defend themselves by chopping the predator's throat, which causes pain and disrupts the predator's airway.

One of the main means of avoiding the Freeze response is to be prepared for it in advance. This can be done through Mind-Setting. Mind-setting is a process used to predetermine your responses to dangerous situations. The concept of Mind-setting is presented by Sanford Strong in his book, '*Strong on Defense: Survival Rules to protect you and Your Family from Crime*' but the principle is widely used in many different arenas. Police and Military organizations might refer to it as Muscle Memory, and some lecturers and speakers utilize a similar technique referred to as Creative Visualization to prepare for their speaking engagements.

The basic concept of Mind-setting is that you determine what you would Probably do if you find yourself in a dangerous situation beforehand (that way you are not making such a critical decision when confronted with a violent crime, while you are experiencing tunnel vision and an adrenal dump that effects your perception). If you find yourself in a dangerous situation, you will be frightened and may be overwhelmed with emotions. To avoid making rash decisions when in such an emotional state, you can use Mind-setting to predetermine your responses and evaluate what options might be available to you. Mind-setting will allow you to make such crucial decisions while in a safe environment (before you are in a dangerous situation).

Mind-setting involves examining previous violent crimes and deciding what you would have done (or will do) if you find yourself in a similar situation. Strong suggests that when watching the news, watching a movie, or when reading a newspaper article dealing with a violent crime, that you take a few minutes and determine what you would have done if you were the victim in the situation. Make a decision and plan out with your family responses to various situations. For example, if reading about a carjacking, you might say to your family that you are going to keep the vehicle doors locked at all times, and that if someone tries to enter the vehicle then you would speed away.

Strong suggests that individuals/families decide before hand what they want to do if faced with an armed robbery, rape, home invasion, or any other violent crime, so that if confronted with such a situation, the individual/family member(s) can take immediate action and respond without requiring lengthy deliberation.

Determining beforehand how you would respond in different violent crime scenarios will provide you with a better understanding of the situation you are in. Knowing what has happened to others, what has worked, and what has failed, will allow you to make the best decision with the information you are given at the time. Of course, there are no correct answers to the situations you might find yourself in, and your actions and responses will be based on how you evaluate the situation you are in when you are in it.

As a veteran police officer, Strong has witnessed the outcome of enough violent crimes to formulate four rules to use when responding to violent crimes. Strong suggests that you should *react immediately*, that you should *resist explosively*, that you should *never go to crime scene number two*, and that you should *never give up*.

Practicing Mind-setting will permit you to act immediately. You can estimate beforehand your chances of survival based on similar crimes you have examined. Immediate reaction prevents the criminal from gaining complete control of the situation. During the opening phases of a confrontation, the perpetrator is seeking to gain control of the situation, and they will attempt to get your cooperation.

During the initial phase of a violent crime, the criminal will often tell you the very thing that you can do to prevent their success. The criminal might say, *"Don't scream"* or, *"Don't run"*, because those are the very actions that can prevent them from gaining the control over you they need in order to accomplish their objectives. Immediate resistance can prevent the perpetrator from gaining control of the situation. Once the perpetrator is in control, they will be more confident, and resistance later will be more difficult.

Resisting immediately prevents the perpetrator from gaining control of the situation. If you were selected by a predator as its prey, then the predator most likely believes he is capable of conquering you without much effort. By resisting immediately, and doing so explosively, you seek to change the predator's perception and make it think it mistakenly attacked another predator.

The third of Strong's four rules is, *"Never go to crime scene #2."* Crime scene number two is the place the criminal wishes to take you to so that they will have you isolated and no one will be able to hear your screams. At that location you will be completely at the perpetrator's mercy, and can expect to be slowly tortured and depending on the type of crime and the criminal's intentions, possibly murdered.

Strong suggests that if you are being taken to crime scene number two, that you crash the car or do anything you can to prevent yourself from going there. The injuries you sustain in a car accident would pale in comparison to what would be done to you at the secondary location. In a sexual assault situation, the rapists will most likely attempt to isolate you before initiating the assault, i.e. you will already be at crime scene number two before the perpetrator tries to assault you.

Strong's final rule of *'never give up'* has to do with your will to survive. When confronted with a violent crime you must continue to fight until the threat is removed (or you escape). Keep fighting until you are safe. No matter how dire the situation seems, even if you are injured, as long as you have life left in your body, do not give up. You can fight through many injuries and during violent situations (when your body goes into its fight, flight, or freeze response) you might not even realize that you've been stabbed or shot until after you've successfully survived the situation.

Being aware of the ability to fight through injuries is important for two reasons. First of all, you must realize that no matter how badly you think you have injured your opponent, you must consider them as a threat until they are no longer capable of attacking you. Secondly, you must realize that even if you become injured, the confrontation is not over, and you must continue to resist until you are clearly out of danger.

During a confrontation you should expect to be injured, so that when you do receive an injury you do not over react, go into shock, and then pass out and bleed to death while you are unconscious. You must maintain the will to fight until the fight is over, and you must ignore your injuries in order to prevent yourself from being injured any further. After the threat to your safety has been eliminated, then you will have time to tend to your wounds.

While still involved in a confrontation, you should focus completely on attacking your opponent until the threat to your safety has been removed. All of the above principles should be included in your Mind-setting. You should decide if and when you wish to resist, you should decide that you are never going to permit yourself to be taken to a secondary location, and you should expect to be injured and must be determined to fight through it.

It is important to keep in mind that the perpetrators have a completely different mentality than you do. You must be careful not to project your values and morals onto the assailant. Do not expect to be able to talk your way out of a violent situation, or to be able to get the perpetrator to see reason. If the perpetrator was reasonable, then he would not be engaging in such activity in the first place. Many rapists are repeat offenders, and if they were unwilling to show mercy to their previous victims, it is very unlikely that they will show mercy to you – regardless of your amount of begging, pleading, or attempts to get them to see reason.

You are extremely unlikely to be able to talk a criminal out of committing a crime, or of being able to decrease the criminal's desire to do so. Your best means of preventing an attack is to decrease the criminal's *opportunity* to target you. You can minimize the _opportunity_ for criminals to target you by remaining aware of their surroundings, and taking precautionary measures in order to become a hard-target.

Perpetrators would not initiate an attack if they did not believe they were capable of succeeding. They must believe they have the _ability_ to pull off their plan. They select their targets based on who they believe they are capable of overpowering, if you find yourself in a violent situation, you are probably already at a disadvantage. The self-defense techniques taught in this section may assist you in escaping or defending yourself, but the techniques will only be effective if they are practiced.

The better prepared you are, the greater your chances of being able to utilize self-defense techniques effectively. However, you must be realistic in expectations. Simply watching a video containing a demonstration of various techniques is not enough to save you. In order for you to utilize defensive techniques effectively, you must be familiar with them – so that you will be able to recall them while in a stressful situation when your body experiences an adrenal dump and you are in an altered state of awareness – and you must practice them, so that the movements are automatic and able to be applied effectively.

You do not need to master all of the techniques in this book, and you might not want to. Select a few techniques that you believe you can utilize successfully, and focus on mastering those techniques. You should practice them to the point that they can be employed through muscle memory – so the movements seem almost automatic. You want to be comfortable and confident in your resistance techniques, otherwise, you might hesitate to use them when you need to.

The techniques provided in this book are not all-inclusive, but are meant to give you a starting point to aid you in escaping. If you want to master the ability to defend yourself, you should regularly attend boxing, martial arts, or other self-defense classes. The techniques provided in this book are Defensive Tactics, meant to provide you with a few techniques that might give you the ability to distract or dissuade an attacker long enough for you to escape. Your objective should be to escape. Out fighting the perpetrator, or attempts to apprehend him, subdue him, or hold him for the police are unlikely to be successful.

Assuming that you master the ability to defend yourself, the skill set of the perpetrator will also be a factor. Your attacker may be relatively harmless and unskilled, which is why he is attacking someone weaker than himself, or he may be a hardened criminal or gang member, who has spent years trying to make himself into a tough guy. The skill set of your opponent, size disparity, or the presence of weapons are all unique factors that must be taken into consideration when deciding whether or not to resist, or what techniques to employ.

The techniques demonstrated in this book seek to exploit weaknesses in the human body, in order to overcome a stronger or more skilled opponent, long enough for you to escape. The decision as to whether or not to attempt these techniques or when to, can only be answered by you, and will be based on the totality of the circumstances you find yourself in.

The first level of resistance in the Use of Force Continuum is Verbal Noncompliance. Ignoring a predator's attempts to manipulate you by refusing to talk with strangers may aid you in avoiding a dangerous situation. If the perpetrator is someone you know, such as a person you are on a date with, your Verbal Noncompliance will be in the form of statements such as *"No", "Stop", "I said No", "This is rape!"* If your attempts at Verbal Noncompliance fail, Passive Resistance – just sitting there – is unlikely to be of any use.

The next level of resistance in the Use of Force Continuum is Active Resistance also known as Escape Resistance, which involves pulling away in an effort to escape. If you are in a position where you are capable of breaking the perpetrator's grip and making a run for it, do so. If you have a screamer, whistle, or other nose making device, set it off, and try to get the attention of witnesses. If you do not have such a device, scream for help.

If you have a cell phone, call 9-1-1, and tell them that someone is trying to rape you, most 9-1-1 dispatchers have the capability of pinging your cell phone to obtain your GPS location, even if your cell phone is not equipped with GPS, 9-1-1 centers may be able to triangulate your cell phone to determine your location. In response to a rape in progress, police will be expedited to your location, depending on your location; help might only be minutes away. If nothing else, phoning 9-1-1 and reporting the rape before it happens will eliminate the possibility of the rapist later claiming the sex was consensual; removing the isolation the perpetrators is seeking to impose on you may cause him to rethink his intent to continue with the attack.

Pressure Point Control Techniques

The first techniques we will discuss are Pressure Point Control Techniques (PPCT), because you might need to use such a technique in order to get the attacker off of you, before you have a chance to run away. In response to being ambushed in a violent attack by a stranger, such techniques would not be appropriate, and more damaging techniques (capable of inflicting a greater degree of bodily harm) may be required in order to escape.

PPCTs might be appropriate, if you are on a date, and are not yet 100% sure that you are in danger or if you do not yet believe a higher amount of force is warranted in the given situation. If your date tries taking things too far, your first attempt might be to Ask'em to stop. If he does not respond to your Verbal Noncompliance, then increase your level of assertiveness, and Tell'em to stop. With authority and conviction, tell him, *"I said no, take your hands off of me, this is rape!"* If the assailant does not respond to you Telling him, then Make'em take his hands off of you.

Ask'em, Tell'em, Make'em. As your level of resistance increases, you will begin to recognize that you are in danger, and the need to defend yourself will become clearer. If your date is ignoring your "No's" and is attempting to rape you, then you must realize that regardless of how you felt about this person previously, if your date is attempting to rape you, then you must realize that there is no hope of you continuing in a relationship with this person, and you should no longer view him as a possible suitor, but as what he is, an evil rapist, who poses an imminent threat to you.

If this is a person that you know, and up until this point, were most likely enamored with, going from shouting "No" to immediately gouging out his eyes may not yet be something you are either ready to do, or at this point, feel is appropriate. If you are unable to push the perpetrator off due to him being stronger than you, you might be able to use PPCT in order to create an opening for you to escape, or as a means of gaining his attention.

There are numerous pressure points on the human body, but in this section, we will limit our discussion to four. You do not need to master all of these points, but try them out on yourself, determine which ones you believe to be the most effective or easiest for you to remember and employ, and focus on mastering those one or two locations.

Pressure Points use pain in order to gain the assailant's compliance. If the techniques do not bring about the desired result, of gaining the assailant's compliance, or if your attempts cause the perpetrator to become more aggressive, you should discontinue their use, and advance to a more effect means of resistance immediately.

The first pressure point we will discuss is located below the nose and above the teeth and is referred to as the Infra Orbital Pressure Point. You can push on this area as a means of causing the perpetrator pain while pushing his face away from you. This can be done seemingly on accident, to make the pain compliance technique seem unintentional. If you chose to use this pressure point, use caution, and be wary of the opponent's mouth – to avoid being bitten.

Infra Orbital Pressure Point

Another pressure point is located behind the jawbone and is known as the Mandibular Angle. To employ this pressure point, push your finger behind the jaw, and press inward, and toward the front of the face. This pressure point could be used in conjunction with the Infra Orbital pressure point, but using the C-clamp technique.

Mandibular Angle Pressure Point

C-Clamp Pressure Point

Another pressure point is located at the bottom of the jaw, approximately an inch forward from point where the jawbone turns from vertical to horizontal. Starting from the back of the jawbone, slide your thumb forward until you find an indention almost the size of the pad of your thumb. To activate this pressure point, push your thumb upward, pushing it up into the skin underneath the jaw and then back towards the bone –known as the Hypoglossal Nerve.

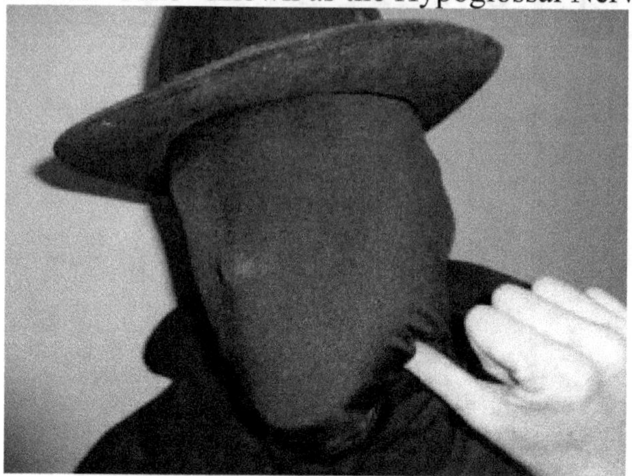

Hypoglossal Nerve Pressure Point

Jugular Notch Pressure Point

The Jugular notch, is an easy point to find, and is located at the base of the neck, where the throat meets the sternum. To activate the Jugular notch, push two fingers into the throat and then downward. All of the aforementioned pressure point techniques should be accompanied by verbal instruction to let you go or for the assailant to back off.

The Use of Force Continuum is not meant to be a step by step escalation of force. You don't need to start out with verbal commands and then climb up the ladder to more aggressive techniques. If a situation warrants deadly force, such as responding to an assailant with a knife, then you do not need to waste your time with verbal commands, followed by pressure points, then strikes, then deadly force techniques. If a situation requires deadly force, then that is the appropriate level of force to use, and you are not required to first attempt a lesser means of response.

The next technique we will discuss is the Wristlock. We will cover two different variations of the wristlock. Wristlocks are useful, because they can immobilize one of your opponent's hands, at least momentarily, which may be employed as a method of gaining control through pain compliance, or as a means of getting the perpetrator into a position where you can push him off of you in order for you to escape.

If employed slowly, wristlocks can be used as a means of gaining pain compliance, but if done rapidly in a snapping motion, you may be able to sprain the person's wrist and take it out of the equation.

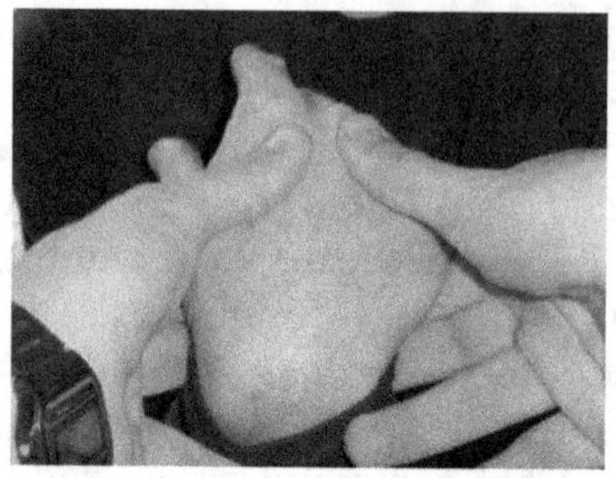 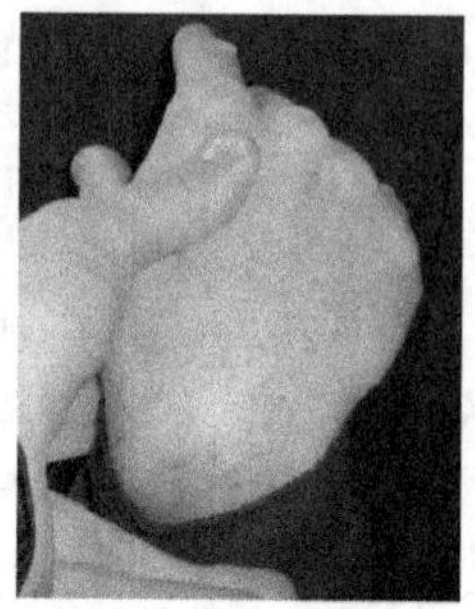

Wristlocks are effective, because regardless of a person's physical strength, the wrist is a weak point that can be exploited by a smaller person in order to injure a stronger person. The secret of the wristlock is proper hand placement. Wristlocks can be accomplished with either a two hand grip, or by using one hand only.

In either case, the grip is the same. To effectively employ a wristlock with two hands, the thumbs should form a triangle, with the fingers providing back pressure on the other side of the assailant's hand. Push forward, towards the opponent with your thumbs and down, and then twist the wrist in either direction. The same grip is used when applying a wristlock with a single hand, as in the above picture.

Unlike Pressure Point Control Techniques, wristlocks are overt, and cannot be claimed to have been applied on accident. If you commit to applying a wristlock, do so wholeheartedly, and with the intent of injuring your opponent. Hopefully, you will disable one of the perpetrator's hands, or be able to push him off of you enough for you to make a run for it. If the wristlock fails, or the perpetrator becomes infuriated by your resistance, you may need to increase your level of resistance immediately – such as by using your thumbs to gouge out the perpetrator's eyes, or the side of your hand to chop the perpetrator's throat.

Regardless of an assailant's physical strength, the eyes and the throat are always vulnerable. Even if someone is wearing body armor and a helmet (as in the photo on the next page) the eyes and the neck remain vulnerable. Attacking your opponent's eyes will disrupt his ability to see you, and may cause him to release his grip or control over you long enough for you to escape. Gouging out a person's eyes may cause permanent blindness, and would be considered serious bodily harm – which equates to deadly force – but such force may be warranted if you feel threatened by an imminent threat of death or serious bodily harm. The Eyes and the Neck are always Vulnerable.

Gouging out your opponent's eyes is not a technique that requires much practice. It can be done by inserting your thumbs into both eyes simultaneously, or you can simply poke your fingers into the assailant's eyes. Gouging an assailant's eyes may not require much precision, but it may require advanced mind-setting, so that you are mentally prepared to do it, if you need to.

Employing such a technique is not a pleasant thought, and may require advanced contemplation in order for you to follow through with it. Eye gouges do not have to be done with your fingers; you can use your keys, a pen, or any items available to you.

Attacking your opponent's throat will disrupt his ability to breath. It will cause him pain, and if you crush his trachea, it may cause death. Such a technique should only be utilized in a life or death situation, when you reasonably believe you are in imminent danger of death or serious bodily harm.

Chops to any part of the neck could be utilized as a means of self-defense. Chopping the trachea is intended to collapse the trachea and disrupt the attacker's ability to breath. It will cause intense pain, which might cause the attacker to loosen his grip on you in order for you to escape. Crushing the trachea could be fatal. Besides chopping the trachea with the edge of your hand, you could also crush it by grabbing it, wrapping your fingers and thumb around the trachea and crushing and twisting it.

Chops to the side of the neck are less effective, but in theory, chops to the carotid arteries are said to force blood into the brain, followed by a period of no blood, which may cause the person to lose consciousness. Striking the side of the neck may also cause the arteries to swell and constrict, which would limit the amount of blood to the brain, which may cause dizziness or disorientation.

Edge of Hand Strike to the Side of the Neck

Spear Hand Strike to the Trachea

Chops to the cervical vertebrae on the back of the neck are referred to as rabbit punches, and if done hard enough, can break the person's neck – causing serious injury or death. A light blow to the back of the neck might cause unconsciousness, or if nothing else, it might cause a distraction and a small amount of pain. Regardless of the technique you use, or the target you attack, you must remember to continue to attack until the fight is over. Even if you successfully strike a target with full force, do not expect the intended results to take place.

You must continue to fight until the fight is over. There is a saying, *'when wrestling a bear, when do you take a break?'* The answer is, when the bear does. If you engage is a physical confrontation, you must be prepared to fight through any injuries you sustain, and continue to fight until the fight is over.

In response to an attempted rape, or anytime you reasonable believe you are in imminent danger of death or serious bodily harm, the eyes and the throat should be your primary targets, as these areas are weaknesses in the human body. They are areas that are not protected by bones or muscle mass, and regardless of how much bigger or stronger your opponent is than you, these areas are a weakness that you can exploit to even the odds. Attacking these areas has the potential of causing death or serious bodily harm, but your objective is only to disrupt the assailant's attack on you, so that you are able to escape and survive the incident.

In response to a rape, attacking the eyes or the throat may be the most appropriate, but having the ability to select from other techniques is useful. Some situations require more than pain compliance techniques and pressure points, but do not require the use of techniques with the potential of causing death or serious injury. Some situations may only require you to punch your opponent. In order to punch effectively, you must practice the techniques. If you do not practice your punches, you probably won't be able to utilize the techniques effectively when you need to.

There are three basic punches in boxing, and once you learn those punches you can modify your techniques slightly in order to fight with a knife. The three basic punches in boxing are the jab, the cross, and the hook. Boxing and Martial Arts are not techniques that you can do one time and expect you use them effective months or years later. To use those techniques effectively, they must be practiced regularly, in order to develop muscle memory.

Even if you are not able to commit to regularly practicing the techniques, any experience or proficiency is better than nothing, and being able to adapt the techniques you've practice in order to wield a knife, will enable you to practice a single technique, which you can modify in order to provide you with more options. You can engage in Active Aggression, by getting into a fist fight, or you can incorporate a knife or blunt object with the techniques you've practiced to engage in Aggravated Active Aggression, or Deadly Force.

Defenses against knives are important, because knives are readily available. They are inexpensive, easy to conceal, and legal to carry on your person. When confronted with a knife wielding assailant, you must be willing to be, and should expect to be cut. If you do get cut or become bloody, you must not let that deter you, and you must remember to continue to fight until the fight is over. You can tend to your wounds after the ordeal, but if you don't remain focused and engaged, you might not survive.

If you wake up to find a knife at your throat, you may be left with no choice but to grab the blade. If you wake up with a knife at your throat, you are already in a horrible situation, being cut on your hand, should be the least of your concerns. Sanford Strong suggests that you grab the blade; it is better to have your hand cut, than it is to have your throat cut. If you lose your grip on the blade, grab it again. While doing this, gouge at the assailant's eyes, chop at his throat, and scream for help. Resist until you are able to escape, or the perpetrator stops his attack. The wristlock techniques described previously can be used as a means of disarming a knife wielding assailant – bending the person's wrist causing him to lose his grip on the knife.

If you find yourself being threatened with a gun, you can use the GOT IT defense. <u>G</u>rab the weapon, move <u>O</u>ut of the line of fire, <u>T</u>wist the weapon, <u>I</u>njure the person of necessary, and <u>T</u>ake the weapon from the assailant.

The majority of information in this chapter was taken directly from the book, *'Hands to War: Fighting, Weapons, and Self-Defense for Christian Families.'* The preceding is meant to provide the reader with an introduction to self-defense concepts, and is not meant to be a complete system of defense. The reader is encourage to explorer other methods and systems, and to adopt and practice techniques and concepts the reader believes she can use effectively and with confidence. Any technique the reader selects should be practiced, and should only be used when appropriate to do so.

Chapter Four

RESPONSE

Unfortunately, despite all of your best efforts or the preventative measures you take, you can do everything right, and still become a victim of sexual assault. You might be overpowered, coerced, drugged, ambushed, manipulated, or in some other way forced to have sexual intercourse without your consent. The fact of the matter is that rapes are a common occurrence throughout the world, and no culture or civilization is able to prevent their occurrence.

Across the globe, an estimated 600,000 to 800,000 men, women, and children are the victims of human trafficking and/or forced into the commercial sex trade at any given time, 70 percent these victims are females and 50 percent are children. According to the Federal Bureau of Investigations' 2010 Crime-Clock, in the United States, a forcible rape occurred every 6.2 minutes. In 2010, more than 84,000 rapes were reported to law enforcement.

If you are the victim of a sexual assault, you must understand and accept the fact that it was not your fault; you did not do anything to deserve it. You have nothing to be embarrassed about, you are not alone, and there are many people out there ready to help you through the challenges that you might face as a result of the assault. Many cities have rape crisis centers or other organizations that may be able to assist you, and can provide you with guidance and support. If the organization in your area has Victims Advocates, then you may want to enlist their assistance.

Victim's Advocates are trained to provide rape victims with support. They should be familiar with the resources that are available to you in your local community. They can answer questions for you, and can assist you in your response and recovery efforts. Victim's Advocates can offer understanding and support that you may not be able to receive from friends or family members.

Your loved ones may be too close to you, to provide you with the support that you need; they may have their own emotions and feelings about the rape that they are trying to process, which may prevent them from giving you the attention and support that you need. Because they love you so much, they may have difficulty dealing with or even thinking about the horror you went through. They may not be able to talk with you about it, and therefore, may not be able to offer you the same level of support that a Victim's Advocate can, as an objective third party.

Even if your friends or family members were able and willing to speak with you about the ordeal and the aftermath you are dealing with, they may lack the training or experience needed to provide you with the necessary answers to your questions. Victim's Advocates, or Survivor Recovery Groups, may be able to provide you with a level of understanding and support that you may not be able to find elsewhere. However, friends, family members, and victim's advocates may all be to provide you with differing levels/types of assistance when responding to and recovering from a sexual assault.

What to do if you are Sexually Assaulted

This section will focus on what to do, immediately following a sexual assault, and what to expect during the processing of evidence and start of a criminal investigation. If you have been sexually assaulted, the first thing you should do is get to a safe place – away from your attacker. The next thing you should do is go to the hospital and seek medical treatment.

Prior to going to the hospital, you may want to phone a Rape Crisis Hotline or your local Sexual Assault Center, because there might be multiple hospitals in your area, but you may need to go to a specific hospital or medical clinic in order to have the Sexual Assault Forensic Examination performed.

Your local organization or rape crisis center will be able to tell you if there is a certain hospital that you need to go to, and they may be able to provide you with a Sexual Assault Victim's Advocate, who can meet you at the hospital and provide you with further assistance and answers your questions. At this point, or once you are at the hospital, you can call a family member or trusted friend for additional support, and/or you can call the police to report the crime.

Once you are safe, you will go to the hospital in order to receive medical treatment, and in order to preserve any forensic evidence. Do not bath, wash up, or change your clothes. Do not brush your teeth, use mouthwash, use the restroom, or treat any of your injuries. Do not eat or drink anything, or take any type of medicine. Do not disturb or clean up the crime scene.

While at the hospital you will be treated for

any injuries you may have sustained, you will be screened for sexually transmitted diseases and pregnancy. A Sexual Assault Forensic Examination will be conducted, and fibers, hairs, saliva, semen, clothing, and other evidence will be collected and stored, in case you decide to prosecute. If you suspect that you were drugged, inform the medical staff, so they can test for that as well. The Forensic Examination is very invasive, and will closely examine your entire body in order to collect evidence – you may be photographed both internally and externally.

The Forensic Examination may take from 3 to 4 hours to complete. The exams are comprehensive, because the victim deserves to be medically protected. It is also important to collect evidence that may be used in a criminal trial. The victim has the right to accept or decline any or all parts of the exam, but it is important to remember that if critical evidence is missed, it will be lost for good. After the evidence is collected, it will be stored in a kit and preserved to aid in a criminal prosecution, if necessary.

Each State will have its own procedures for processing and storing evidence. In the State of Kansas, medical facilities are prohibited from notifying the police about a sexual assault without first obtaining written consent from the victim. Kits that are not turned over to the police are stored by the State for a period of five years, giving the victim time to decide whether or not she wishes to report the assault and prosecute the offender.

The decision as to whether or not to report or prosecute the crime does not have to be made immediately following the attack. By undergoing the

Sexual Assault Forensic Examination, the victim will have time to decide what she wishes to do, once she has had time to process what has happened – immediately following a sexual assault is not the time to make such an important decision. However, collecting evidence (to keep the option open) and ensuring your medical safety are important, and cannot be put off for a later date. In Kansas, the county in which the assault occurred will pay for the forensic examination.

Besides collecting forensic evidence, and treating the victim's injuries, the medical staff will also discuss and/or test for pregnancy and Sexually Transmitted Disease (STDs). If you take birth control pills, your chance of pregnancy is small, but if you do not take them, you may consider a pregnancy prevention treatment. Pregnancy prevention consists of taking 2 estrogen pills when you first get to the hospital, and 2 more about 12 hours later. This treatment may reduce the risk of pregnancy by 60-90%.

There is a 5-10% chance of contracting a STD as the result of a sexual assault. Your doctor can prescribe medicine to treat for STDs as well. Your odds of getting HIV as the result of a rape are less than 1%, but you can be tested for it for your peace of mind.

The forensic evidence collected during the medical examination documents sexual contact, but does not prove that a rape occurred. If you desire justice, you will need to report the assault to law enforcement, and work with the justice system in an effort to prosecute the perpetrator.

Reporting the incident can aid in preventing

future crimes; rapists will continue in their behavior until they are stopped. You deserve justice, and in order to reduce the epidemic number of rapes that regularly occur around the world, we must prosecute and prevent rapists from continuing to victimize others. While there is no way to change what happened to you, you can pursue justice, and help stop it from happening to someone else. Taking rapists off the street is the most effective means of preventing future rapes, but ultimately, the choice to report the crime and seek justice can only be made by the victim.

There is a difference between reporting the assault and pressing charges. The victim may not be emotionally ready to press charges immediately following a police report, but contacting the police as soon as possible after a sexual assault will afford them with the best opportunity to collect evidence and conduct a successful investigation. In some instances, the prosecutor will move forward with charges based solely on the evidence that is available.

In sexual assault cases, the crime is prosecuted in criminal court, with the State acting as the prosecuting party. The defendant is prosecuted for violating the laws of the State, and the sexual assault victim, is a witness on behalf of the State. Whether or not the case can move forward will depend on if the prosecution is able to prove non-consent, based on corroborating evidence from the forensic evidence and/or witnesses. If the prosecution does not feel they can prove the defendant's guilt beyond a reasonable doubt, they may not move forward with the case.

Prosecutors understand the difficulties survivors of sexual assault would face while going through a jury trial, and rather than expose the victim to cross examination, they may seek a plea bargain, and may permit the defendant to plead guilty to a lesser crime in order to avoid making the victim testify during a jury trial. The plea bargain may allow the perpetrator to plead guilty in exchange for a lighter sentence or they may plead guilty to a lesser crime.

Approximately 95% of convictions are obtained as the result of plea bargains. By examining the available evidence, the prosecutor can project the likelihood of a conviction, and will offer a plea agreement based upon the likelihood of a successful conviction. Though the offender may avoid the maximum sentence, plea agreements at least provide the victim with some level of justice, and do so while avoiding the need to re-traumatize the victim by having her every action scrutinized during a jury trial.

In some situations, the prosecutor may not have enough evidence to successfully prosecute the case; in such a situation, it doesn't mean that the prosecutor does not believe that the victim was raped. It simply means that there isn't enough evidence to successfully convict the perpetrator. To improve the amount of evidence and to increase the likelihood of a successful prosecution, the sexual assault victim should be completely honest and candid during the initial investigation by law enforcement.

The initial police report may be conducted by a patrol officer in response to a 9-1-1 call. Following the initial report, the case may be assigned to Detectives, who will conduct an extensive and very explicit and personal interview with the victim and with any witnesses. The crime scene will also be processed, and detectives will seek to corroborate the victim's statements and other evidence collected.

The perpetrator may not be arrested immediately, and investigators may need to corroborate evidence in order to establish probably cause for an arrest. Prior to an arrest, the perpetrator may be interviewed as part of the investigation, and his version of events may also need to be investigated before an arrest can be made. To assist officers in establishing probably cause to arrest the assailant, answer the investigator's questions candidly and in painful detail. Doing so will assist investigators in profiling the offender and may aid in obtaining a confession during an interrogation.

If the perpetrator was a stranger, providing candid detail can aid investigators in profiling the rapist. The things the rapist says or does during the assault, can aid investigators is profiling the rapist, which may aid them in identifying a suspect if the rapist's identity is unknown, or it may aid in the interrogation of the suspect.

If the investigators have a psychological profile of the rapist, they can tailor their method of interrogation to enhance their ability to obtain a confession. If investigators are able to garner a confession to the crime, then prosecution of the crime is much easier, and obtaining a plea agreement and avoiding a trial much more likely. However, in order to profile the offender, investigators will need to obtain detailed information from the victim during their interview.

The interview should be conducted in a safe place, where the victim feels comfortable. Investigators will need to be patient with the victim, due to the effects of trauma, which may cause difficulty in remembering the exact sequence of events, gaps in memory, or the inability to remember certain aspects of the assault. A good interviewer should express regret to the victim, assure her that it was not her fault, and assure her of her safety.

The investigator should remind the victim, that it is not illegal to go out with someone and have a few beers, but it is illegal for someone to force non-consensual sex on her. They should explain why they need to ask the questions, and both investigators and the victim need to utilize the same terminology to describe either body parts or sexual acts.

The behavior of the rapist will aid in the construction of a profile. What did the rapist say or do? Did he make threats, use profanity? What type of physical force was used? What sexual acts occurred? Investigators will need to explore the assault in as much detail as possible. They need to prove, based on corroborated evidence that the perpetrator violated the State statutes that constitute rape.

They will need to show resistance and/or non-consent. Did the victims say "No", fight back, was she threatened, beaten, overpowered, in an altered state of consciousness? Are there bruises or corroborating evidence to support the victim's account of the events? How did the perpetrator gain control of the victim? What was the victim feeling, thinking, doing, saying, during the attack? Answers to those questions can help establish non-consent.

The investigators need to portray force, non-consent, and other aspects of the assault, which clearly present the incident as a rape – as defined by the State's statutes. Well-written police reports can change a jury trial into a bench trial or a bench trial into a plea agreement. Knowing exactly what happened, will assist investigators in corroborating the victim's account, while interviewing the assailant, and the investigators can identify how and when the perpetrator starts trying to deceive them when telling his version of events. The more information investigators have prior to an interview or interrogation, the better their chances of obtaining a confession, or if nothing else, corroborating evidence during their interrogation of the perpetrator.

Nothing about this process is going to be easy. The decision as to whether or not to report a sexual assault or to try to prosecute one is not something that should be taken lightly. The period immediately following a rape is a very traumatic and emotional time, and at that point, recounting the rape in gory detail to a number of complete strangers such as law enforcement officers, prosecutors, doctors, advocates, friends, and family members is probably the last thing the victim will want to do.

However, after having had a chance to process what has happened, and once in a safe place, the sexual assault survivor may want to seek the justice they deserve (or may want to do so at some point in the future during her recovery). To ensure this opportunity is not lost, a Sexual Assault Forensic Exam should be conducted, and evidence should be collected and stored – ensuring that the victim will have the option of reporting and/or prosecuting the crime, if she decides to do so some time in the future.

– Chapter Five –

RECOVERY

Being the victim of rape, childhood sexual abuse, or any other type of sexual assault can be devastating and life shattering. Every person is unique, and will respond differently to the various traumas they might have been exposed to. There is no single formula for recovery that will work for everyone, because there are so many different variables and life experiences that go into making each person's reaction distinctive.

The impact on a survivor of long-term childhood sexual abuse will be different than how someone with a supportive family, healthy relationships, and a solid support system might respond to a single date rape that occurs in her early 20s. A victim of childhood sexual assault may have his or her understanding of sexual roles and behavior, and even his/her entire worldview formulated or influenced by the abuse. He/she may grow up not feeling entitled to say "no" to sex, and/or may have developed a multitude of coping mechanisms in order to survive the abuse, which may now be maladaptive coping mechanisms that may be causing the survivor problems in his/her adult life. Survivors of a single rape may have a better baseline as to what should be acceptable behavior regarding their sexuality, but they too may be devastated by a sexual assault.

This chapter is not meant to provide survivors of sexual assault with a step-by-step formula for recovery; that is far outside of the scope of this book, and in all actuality, a step-by-step method that will work for everyone does not exist. There are many different types of cognitive, behavioral, psychological, and other types of therapies available to survivors, but determining which type of therapy will work best for a particular survivor is a personal decision that can only be answered by the individual.

Though each person's response to therapy may be different, there are some common responses to sexual assault that are shared by many survivors. This chapter is not meant to provide therapeutic advice, but seeks to provide the reader with an understanding of some of the types of symptoms, issues, and/or responses a victim of sexual assault might experience.

If you are the victim of a sexual assault, there is nothing anyone can do to erase or undue what has happened to you. However, you do not need to let your victimization define you. You may have been victimized, but you do not have to remain a victim. You can become a survivor.

The term 'Survivor', is a preferred expression used to describe a former victim of sexual assault. Survivors are people who refuse to remain a victim. They choose to move forward with their lives, and seek to overcome any triggers, fears, or other side effects or challenges they experience as the result of a sexual assault. Survivors seek to take their lives back. There is nothing anyone can do to remove the fact that this horrible thing has happened to them, but Survivors will not allow their previous victimizations to define them or their futures.

Every person is unique and will respond differently to a sexual assault, but there are some common responses the reader should be aware of. The information in this section will provide an overview of some of the common responses victims and survivors may experience following a sexual assault (or childhood sexual abuse). Not every person will experience all of these symptoms, but being aware of the various possible responses may assist survivors in identifying traits, triggers, or emotional responses that they may wish to address in therapy.

The trauma experienced by a sexual assault is profound, and survivors deserve to regain control of their lives. They have the right to feel safe in their own bodies, and should be allowed to experience life without constant feelings of fear, anxiety, or hyper-vigilance. Knowing about some of the possible side effects or responses that may occur following a rape, may assist in a person in understanding the phenomena they might be experiencing. However, they should not feel they need to compartmentalize or process the trauma they experienced all on their own.

Survivors deserve to regain control over their lives and emotions, and deserve to be supported in their efforts. If you are the Survivor of a sexual assault, you owe it to yourself to get support and assistance in overcoming the challenges you might face during your recovery. Survivors should be encouraged to seek professional help, and should explore the different types of therapies and support systems available to them, until they find something that works for them.

If the survivor is not interested in seeking the help of a professional, then she should consider joining a support group, with other survivors, who may be able to provide advice as to how they overcame or dealt with similar challenges. A trusted friend or family member may also be able to provide support. A Sexual Assault Victim's Advocate may be able to direct a victim to resources available in the local community.

The bottom line is that if you (or someone you know) are the victim of a sexual trauma, you do not have to deal with it alone. There are resources and skilled professionals that may provide you with comfort, or may assist you in processing or overcoming the challenges you might be experiencing.

The effects of Rape or Childhood Sexual Abuse can be devastating, and can alter the way the survivor responds to situations in his or her daily life from that point forward. Survivors who seek professional help, may be diagnosed with Post Traumatic Stress Disorder, Rape Trauma Syndrome, or various other classifications, but regardless of how the experience is defined, the survivor will be confronted with many different emotions, and responses as the result of being sexually assaulted.

Survivors may experience depression, guilt, shame, fear, anxiety, stress, anger, and other profound emotions, and they may develop any number of maladaptive coping mechanisms, or negative responses to stimuli in future situations. Survivors may experience flashbacks or triggers, and survivors of childhood sexual abuse may experience additional challenges. Recovering from a sexual assault is a process that begins immediately after the threat has ended, but the effects of the trauma can be widespread and experienced differently as time goes by.

Immediately after the assault, the victim may experience pain, nausea, vomiting, headaches, and may have physical injuries that will need to heal. She may experience shock or denial, feel numb or apathetic, socially withdrawn, have difficulty concentrating, irritability, disassociation, a low self-esteem, a lack of security, or an inability to trust others. She may feel guilt, shame, embarrassment, have a loss of appetite, thoughts of suicide, insomnia, nightmares, hyper-vigilance, panic attacks, or sexual dysfunction. The victim may develop eating disorders, substance abuse problems, or engage in self-mutilation. Of course, not all survivors will experience all of these effects, but they may experience a number of them and/or they may experience different effects at different stages of their recovery.

After any violent crime, a sense of fear and a

feeling of loss of personal safety may be one of the first issues that may need to be addressed. Following a sexual assault, extra precautions should be taken to help the survivor feel safe. The victim may need someone to stay with her during for the first few days or weeks after an assault.

Triggers and Flashbacks

As time goes on, the survivor may regain her sense of safety, but certain events or situations may trigger the survivor, which may cause panic attacks, a feeling of hyper-vigilance, nightmares, or flashbacks. Triggers can be caused by anything, a touch, a smell, a sound, or any other stimulus that reminds the survivor of the assault – causing flashbacks, or producing profound emotions, such as fear, depression, guilt, shame, and so on. Triggers are a major issue that many survivors are plagued with.

In an effort to avoid triggers, survivors may withdraw from their usual activities, avoid certain places, smells, people, and so on. They may develop maladaptive coping strategies, which cause them to avoid more and more situations and stimuli until the victim places herself into a small box, where she attempts to hide from the world, and becomes trapped in a prison of her own making; scared to go into certain rooms, leave the house, go to work, or engage in activities.

Hiding from the world or dissociating is not the answer. Survivors have already been forced to endure a horrible event(s), to allow the aftereffects of the trauma(s) to impact the person's freedom of movement or ability to enjoy her life is not fair.

Triggers are a challenge that many survivors may face, but it is important that the survivors do not allow their triggers to control their behavior. If you are having trouble in this area, seek professional help. You deserve to feel safe, and you deserve to live your life on your own terms, and to not be controlled or defined by the things that have happened to you in the past.

Triggers, Flashbacks, and Intrusive Memories are a common reaction to trauma, and may cause the survivor to re-live what happened, or to re-experience certain aspects or feelings associated with the trauma; such as the intense fear or feelings of impending death or helplessness the person may have experienced during the assault.

Many of the techniques utilized to reduce anxiety can also be used to cope with flashbacks and triggers. Positive suggestions or affirmations might be employed, hypnosis or breathing exercises, creative visualization, or EMDR are just some of the techniques that are available. EMDR stands for Eye Movement Desensitization and Reprocessing, and is a form of psychotherapy that some people find effective in processing traumatic events such as rape, and is also used to assist war veterans with PTSD.

If one method or technique is not successful, do not give up. Try something else, and keep trying until you find something that works for you. You deserve happiness and liberty in your life. One of the more challenging things about triggers is that you might not know what exact stimulus is triggering the response. It may take a careful examination of multiple situations where you were triggered to find a common factor or identify the triggering event.

Creative Visualization

Creative Visualization may be combined with breathing exercises, and used as a means of self-hypnosis to effect changes in your sub-conscious mind. Triggers are basically Conditioned Responses, and work similar to how Pavlov utilized Classical Conditioning to cause his dogs to salivate each time they heard a bell ring. Pavlov's experiment involved ringing a bell to alert his dogs that it was time to eat, and through this conditioning, the dogs began connecting the ringing of the bell with mealtime. The conditioning caused a physiological change to take place within the dogs, so that whenever the dogs heard the bell, they would begin to salivate, as their bodies began preparing to eat.

Triggers work in the same manner, but the conditioning occurred more rapidly, because the Triggers were formulated during a time of intense emotion. Since Triggers are similar to Conditioned Responses, if not synonymous with them, various methods of Behavioral Modification can be employed to assist in dealing with them.

As an example, a breathing exercise can be combined with self-hypnotic suggestions, or creative visualization, in an effort to control your fear, cope with the trigger, or modify a certain behavior. Creative Visualization involves visualizing yourself the way that you want to be or wish you were. If you were traumatized in the backseat of a car or in a dark closest, those places might trigger the feelings or emotions you associate with those places, thereby making you afraid of the dark, or causing you to avoid automobiles.

To utilize Creative Visualization to modify

those conditioned responses, you might visualize yourself in the backseat of the car or in a dark closet, but feeling totally comfortable and confident. When you visualize those images, create those feelings and emotions to accompany the visualizations. Make it as real as possible. Your objective is to pair the new feelings and emotions you'd like to experience in those situations, in order to replace the triggers or negative conditioning that is currently associated with those places or situations.

Creative Visualization is not limited to modifying triggers, but can be used to prepare for other things, such as job interviews, speaking engagements, and other stress management related situations. If you are one of those people who find visualization difficult, you can achieve the same (or similar) results by using positive affirmations or self-hypnotic suggestions.

In order to do so, you would begin with a breathing exercise, just as you would if you were going to practice Creative Visualization. By closing your eyes and focusing on rhythmic breathing, you can enter a light trance state where your sub-conscious mind is open to suggestions, and can be reprogrammed with the thoughts and ideas that you want – that may be more beneficial to you.

A trance state is easy to achieve, and within a few minutes of rhythmic breathing you will be in an altered state of consciousness that is sufficient to reprogram your sub-conscious mind with positive suggestions or self affirmations. Keep your suggestions positive, in the present tense, and focused on what you do want, and do not focus on the things you want to avoid. Do not think negative thoughts to yourself such as, *"I'm such a failure"*, and likewise, avoid making statements that focus on the negative, such as, *"the next time I have to give a speech, I won't get all sick and throw up"*. Instead, focus on what you do want, and on the behavior you wish to embrace. Your affirmations should be more along the line of, *"I am a smart, confident, and capable person, I trust my instincts and intuition, I am prepared, I can and will protect myself, I deserve respect and will protect my boundaries, and I am confident in my ability to do so."*

Once you gain access to your sub-conscious mind, you can effect changes in it, and modify your behavior through either self affirmations, or through creative visualization. Either technique can be effective; the method you select is simply a personal preference. There are many methods to bring about a trance state, but in this example, we will discuss rhythmic breathing.

To perform rhythmic breathing, you would close your eyes, and take a deep breath as you count up to eight, you would then hold your breath for the count of four, then exhale for the count of eight, and then repeat the process. This technique is also referred to as 8-4-8 breathing, but the numbers are not important. You can use 6-3-6 or any other combination of numbers. The objective is simply to concentrate on your breathing as you take slow deep relaxing breaths.

You can incorporate other things into the exercise to aid in your concentration, such as breathing in through your nose and out through your mouth, or by visualizing that you are inhaling a color or mist, and exhaling a different color. You can time your breaths to the heart rate, by counting one number with each beat of your heart. The purpose of the breathing exercise is for you to relax, and enter a state of focused concentration where you can make changes to the conditioning in your sub-conscious mind.

Grounding

Another method for dealing with flashbacks and triggers is referred to as Grounding. Grounding is a process of reorientation, where you remind yourself that although you may be experiencing the same fear, terror, or other associations with a time when you were being traumatized or abused, the events are <u>NOT HAPPENING NOW</u>. You are only experiencing a memory, and in your present situation, you are safe.

Various methods of grounding can be employed, and like other therapies or techniques, determining what works best for you will be based on personal preference. Some people try to shock their bodies by taking an ice cold shower, or sucking on an ice cube. Others use smells or aromas to bring them back to the present. Grounding involves focusing on a sensation in the here and now to counteract the triggered emotional responses you might be experiencing. Self-affirmations might also be used as part of grounding, such as, *"That was then; this is now. Now I am in a safe place, now I am in control of my body."*

Some survivors experience disassociation when triggered. They may have developed a coping mechanism of disassociating from their body during abuse or while being sexually assaulted. When being abused, they may have left their bodies or retreated into a mental world, so as not to be aware of what was happening to them.

When these people are triggered, they may begin to disassociate from their bodies, and may need to wiggle their toes, stand up and walk around, or find some other way of grounding themselves and remaining present in their bodies. They might hold a certain item, pet their dog or cat, rub their feet on the ground, call a friend, turn on the lights and look around the room, listen to music, or practice a breathing exercise.

Triggers and flashbacks can be a challenge, but they are a normal phenomenon that many survivors experience. When a trigger or flashback occurs, the survivor may need to be grounded and to remind herself that she is safe. Keeping a journal and documenting the triggers may aid in identifying the causes of the triggers, or in processing the assault. Once the person is grounded and in the present (and feels safe), she may write in a journal or engage in Creative Visualization or Self-Hypnosis in an effort to modify the conditioned response that was triggered.

Triggers and Flashbacks may be experienced by Rape Survivors, and by Survivors of Childhood Sexual Abuse. The two categories of survivors may experience many of the same emotional responses to the sexual traumas they have experienced.

Responses to Sexual Assaults

Guilt and Shame are common responses among both

sexual assault and child sexual abuse survivors. A survivor of childhood sexual abuse may feel guilty about the abuse he or she endured, because their abuser may have convinced them that it was their fault. Some Child Molesters purposely shame or humiliate their victims in order to keep them silent, and to prevent their victims from reporting the crime.

They groom their victims beforehand; manipulate them during the time period when the abuse occurs, and afterwards, in order to keep their victims quiet. Victims might be told that it was their fault, that they wanted it, made the perpetrator do it, that if anyone found out they would not be believed, or that the child's family would blame them.

Children might also be threatened, and told that if they tell then their victimizer would kill them, kill their parents, or that they would be responsible for destroying their family (if one of the family members is taken off to jail for being the perpetrator). The survivor of Childhood Sexual Abuse my feel dirty, have a low self-esteem, believe they were born bad, or that the things they are forced to endure is the result of them being bad or worthless.

Survivors of Childhood Sexual Abuse may feel a great degree of guilt or shame, because when they were in a fragile time of their childhood, they were exposed to horrible things, and may have been manipulated or told straight-out by their abuser that the abuse was their fault and that they were to blame for it.

Survivors of a Rape or other Sexual Assault may feel guilt or shame about their behavior or their actions leading up to the assault. They might second guess their actions, and contemplate that the rape occurred because of the way they were dressed, the place they went, the fact that they were drinking or using drugs, or that they might have led their attacker on. None of which is true.

The majority of rapes are preplanned, and the rapist intends on assaulting his victim regardless of what the person was wearing. Drinking, isolation, and other factors were not the fault of the victim, but were more than likely orchestrated by the rapist(s) in order to set the person up to be assaulted. Drinking and partying is not a crime. The only person who commits a crime during a sexual assault is the rapist. Trusting the wrong person or behaving is a certain manner does not justify being sexually assaulted.

When a sexual assault occurs, the blame always rests with the rapists. The survivor can do everything perfectly correct, and still fall victim to a rapist. The rapist has put a lot of thought into his plan, and he manipulates events in order to facilitate the assault. The victim is not solely focused on the possibility that someone might attack her, and is only able to respond well into the rapist's trap, and is left with very limited options.

Shame and Guilt are unwarranted and serve only to deepen the trauma. Survivors must understand, that regardless of what they wore, said, or did, nothing could justify them being sexually assaulted, and the blame, shame, and guilt, should always be placed on the perpetrator. The Sexual Assault was not the victim's fault.

The Natural Response to Simulation

Some survivors feel guilt or shame because they don't

understand certain aspects of the human body. The human body is designed to have sex, and sex is a natural function. The fact that a perpetrator forces an unnatural sexual act on his victim does not change the fact that our bodies are designed to response to sexual stimulus.

One rape myth is that a male cannot be raped by a female, because *'he must want it in order to get an erection.'* This myth is inaccurate, because <u>the human body is designed to respond to sexual stimulus</u>. If a molester fondles an adolescent's genitals, there will be a response. If the victim was a boy and his victimizer a man, this might cause the abused boy to question his sexuality – he might assume he must be a homosexual, or that he must have wanted to be the victim of child molestation, which could not be further from the truth.

Some female rape victims have felt guilt or shame, because they became wet or had an orgasm while being gang raped. The fact of the matter is that these are natural responses to sexual stimuli, and your body responds that way, because that is how you were made. Certainly, no person would want to be gang raped or molested, but rape myths and a lack of understanding of how the human body naturally responds to stimulus can cause some survivors to experience shame or guilt about things that were completely out of their control, and are not an accurate reflection of their true intentions.

Child Molesters and other sexual predators may exploit their victim's natural responses in an attempt to convince their victim that the assault was really the victim's fault or that the victim must have really wanted it; this is done on purpose, in an effort to prevent the victim for reporting the incident.

Anxiety, Fear, and Stress

Anxiety is experienced by the majority of sexual assault survivors. Many survivors experience a sense of hyper-vigilance and a need to always be on guard – as if they might be sexually assaulted again at any moment. They may experience constant stress, have headaches, nausea, or panic attacks, and the constant sense of hyper-vigilance and stress can be extremely taxing on the body; causing them to feel fatigued.

They may develop fears of being alone or fear leaving their house. Triggers can bring about a sense of fear or panic, and such episodes may cause the survivor to have anxiety, stress, or fear about the possibility of being triggered when out in public. Journaling might be one way to document the feelings of fear and anxiety, and may assist the survivor in identifying ways to face her fears or to work through them.

Anger

Anger and irritability are another common side effect to rape or sexual abuse. Survivors have a right to be angry, but they must be careful not to direct the anger at themselves. The assault was not their fault, and the rightful recipient of their anger is the attacker. However, aside from aiding law enforcement in the investigation and prosecution of the attacker, the anger towards the perpetrator may be left with no outlet.

The stress and fatigue the survivor is experiencing coupled with their anger and irritability may cause them to lash out as those around them. Anger is a powerful emotion that the survivor is justified in feeling, but he or she may need to seek the help of a professional to assist them in providing an acceptable outlet for this emotion – so the survivor can release the anger in a manner that is not harmful to herself or her loved ones. Breathing exercises might be one tool that can aid in reducing stress and managing the emotions, or perhaps exercise or engaging in some other activity.

Trust

The inability to trust is another effect of sexual assault that many survivors encounter. Perpetrators of sexual assault will often exploit their victim's trust in order to set them up to be assaulted. In cases of Child Molestation, the molester is usually a parent, family member, or trusted friend that breaks faith and violates an otherwise trusting relationship in order to sexual abuse his victim.

Rebuilding a sense of trust is difficult when the person or persons you trust most in the world takes advantage of your trust and uses it to violate you. It is natural for survivors of sexual assault to be cautions or suspicious of others, until the person is able to prove his or her trustworthiness. Being suspicious is okay, after all, it is your safety on the line, and your safety is more important than another person's feelings.

Trusting others is not necessary in many situations, but certain people – such as your spouse and children – you will want to build a trusting relationship with. Such people are most likely your loved ones; they should be understanding about your difficulties with trust, and should be patient and willing to work with you.

Helplessness

Some survivors feel powerlessness or a sense of helplessness. They have been deprived of their basic human dignity, and experienced a situation in which they were not even allowed to feel safe in or to have control of their own body. Victims of childhood sexual abuse may have been led to believe that they do not have control of what is done to their bodies, and they may grow up feeling powerless and unable to decline the sexual advances of another person.

This sense of helplessness is often linked to a person's self-esteem, and the survivor may feel dirty, worthless, unable to stand up for herself, and completely at the mercy of the perpetrator. Survivors of rape are forced to endure the sexual assault, and they experience a complete loss of control. During the survivor's recovery, she should be allowed to make her own decisions, and loved ones should not second guess the decisions she makes.

Everything has been taken from the survivor, allowing her to make her own decisions lets her take the first few steps in regaining control of her life. Friends and family members need to permit the survivor to make her own decisions, and should avoid influencing the survivor on matter such as whether or not to report the crime or to prosecute the offender. Receiving medical treatment and collecting forensic evidence are important, but the ultimate decision on reporting the crime to the police is a decision that only the victim can make.

Safety

Following a sexual assault, the survivor will need a safe place to recover, and may need a trusted friend or family member to stay with her and to reassure her in the beginning. Installing a burglar alarm, new locks, getting a dog and/or other safety measures may provide the survivor with a greater sense of security, but fear, panic attacks, triggers, and hyper-vigilance may still take place for some time.

Grounding or stress management techniques may assist in overcoming unwarranted fears. Fear and intuition is a powerful warning device that humans possess instinctually. Fear can be compared to a burglar alarm and goes off to make us aware of a possible danger. Once the alarm has gone off, we can address the situation, and we no longer need the alarm to continue to sound. Fear is a powerful tool that can warn us of the possibility of danger, but if there is no threat, then the emotion of fear is not warranted.

Fear is an emotion that should be embraced and controlled. We want the fear response to alert us to possible dangers, but once we are alerted to a danger, we do not want to continue to stand there frozen with fear. Mind-Setting can be incorporated with the Creative Visualization or Self-Hypnosis techniques discussed previously as a way to train ourselves to utilize fear appropriately. We want to receive the warning single, but then turn it off so that we can take action and address the cause of the alarm.

Sexual Intimacy

Rape is not about sex. Rape is about power and control. When a rape occurs, sex is not the motivation; sex is the weapon that is used. However, since the actions so closely mimics the natural sexual functions of the human body, it may be difficult for survivors to distinguish between rape and healthy sexual intimacy.

Attempts at loving intimacy may cause the survivor to be triggered, disassociate, or experience negative emotions. After a sexual assault, couples may need to ease back into their sexual relationship, and may need to stop in the middle of intercourse in order for the survivor to ground herself into the present.

Regaining sexual intimacy is a challenge, but it is worth it. The survivor deserves to live life to its fullest, and should not be deprived of any pleasure, simply because some evildoer forced her to experience a trauma in her past. Couples should speak openly with each other and express their concerns. Seeking professional assistance from a counselor with experience in dealing with sexual trauma may be necessary. It might be that couples need to avoid certain sexual acts, or to make other concessions such as not doing it late at night or leaving the lights on during intercourse, in order to ease back into a healthy sexual relationship.

Sexual Promiscuity

Another possible issue relating to sexual intimacy is sexual promiscuity. The survivor may attempt to use sex as a coping mechanism. This might be done in an unconscious effort at impulsion therapy. Impulsion Therapy is a Behavioral Modification technique where a person seeks to overcome his/her fears, such as a fear of snakes, by being locked in a room full of snakes.

Impulsion Therapy is an attempt at desensitization. Sexual Promiscuity may be a maladaptive coping mechanism in which the victim seeks to make the sexual act meaningless in her mind, by engaging in promiscuous behavior in order to cheapen the experience. If having sex does not matter, then maybe the rape will not seem as important.

In another variation of the sexual promiscuity coping mechanism, survivors may engage in sexual activity they do not want in an effort to avoid being raped again. The idea is that if the person finds herself in a situation where she feels threatened by the possibility of unwanted sex, then it may seem preferable to her to consent to the unwanted sexual contact than to be raped again. In the survivor's mind, being a slut is better than being a victim, because at least by submitting, she can maintain some sense of control.

Some survivors may avoid future sexual conduct, or they may become sexually promiscuous as a means of minimizes the sexual assault. If sex becomes meaningless, then maybe she can convince herself that the rape was unimportant also, or the person may engage in or initiate sex as a self-preservation strategy to avoid being raped (as a means of maintain a sense of control). Sexual promiscuity is a maladaptive coping mechanism that will only bring the person more pain, shame, and heartache in the long run. Substance abuse or becoming addicted to drugs are other maladaptive behaviors that a victim might engage in, hoping to deal with her trauma, only to have her troubles compounded.

The aforementioned effects represent some of the possible responses survivors of sexual assault or childhood sexual abuse may experience immediately after the assault or at some point during their recoveries. The list is not all inclusive; each survivor is unique and may not experience some of the effects, or they may experience other side effects not mentioned in this chapter. Victims of childhood sexual abuse may experience additional aftereffects, and rape victims may also experience some of the following.

Childhood Sexual Abuse

Survivors of Childhood sexual abuse may experience additional aftereffects, because the abuse may have occurred before the child possessed a full understanding of how the world works, and what constitutes appropriate and inappropriate behavior. Survivors of childhood sexual abuse may have been deprived of their basic human dignity and treated not as a human being, but as an outlet for someone else's sexual desires.

Such victims may grow into adulthood not believing they are entitled to say, *'No'* to sex, and/or may feel completely helpless, dirty, bad, worthless, or have almost no self-esteem at all. Most of these children fall through the cracks, and end up experiencing further victimization as they get older. They may try to escape into a world of drugs and alcohol, or end up committing suicide, dying of AIDS, or surviving on the streets as a prostitute.

In her book, *'Secret Survivors: Uncovering Incest and Its Aftereffects in Women'*, Blume provides a Incest Survivors Aftereffects Checklist, and then goes through each item and explains how these aftereffects or maladaptive coping strategies may be adversely effecting survivors of incest and childhood sexual abuse well into their adult lives.

There are 34 items in Ms Blume's list; we will only cover a few of them in this chapter. If you or someone you know seems to fit into one of these aftereffects, then perhaps recognizing the possibility of the behavior being linked to previous abuse may assist the survivor in seeking help.

Not feeling at home or comfortable in one's own body, or attempting to manipulate body's size are two possible aftereffects. Female survivors of childhood sexual abuse may feel that they were victimized because of their gender, and secretly wish they were a male. As a child, she might have fantasized that as she grew older, she would turn into a boy, and then the abuse would stop. This hope to escape abuse by changing genders may be affecting the survivor's sexuality as an adult. She might not feel like a woman, or be resistant to expressing feminine traits or behavior, such as wearing women's clothing or putting on make-up.

Others might have come to believe that the abuse was caused by their attractiveness or small stature. In an attempt to remedy this, as an adult the person might overeat in an effort to be less attractive or to gain 'body armor.' Each of these coping mechanisms is maladaptive, and the survivor should seek professional assistance in overcoming these issues.

Being overweight is not healthy, and sexual confusion may cause unnecessary turmoil in the survivor's life. The fact of the matter is that Child Molesters seek out victims they believe they can successfully victimize. The child is targeted for its vulnerability, and not because of its gender or physical appearance.

Some survivors develop a *'Pattern of victimization';* victims of childhood sexual abuse learn to be victims, and unfortunately, other predators that are looking for victims, are good as recognizing potential victims. The victims may lack the ability to set limits or say no. Until the victim is taught self-worth, self-esteem, boundaries, and given back control of their own bodies, they may continue to fall victim to predators indefinitely.

They may have sexual issues. Sex may feel 'dirty' or they may have an aversion to being touched or showing affection. They may have a particular aversion to certain sexual acts, or they may have a need to engage in particular sexual acts.

They might engage in S&M, or feel the need to remain in either a dominant or submissive role during sex. They may become sex-a-holics and become promiscuous as a means of gaining control of their sexuality (or feeling like they are in control), even though they are working in a field that is clearly exploiting and further abusing them, such as being a porn star, prostitute, escort, or stripper. They may engage in promiscuous impersonal sexual contacts with complete strangers, while being unable to engage in sexual activity with their partner/spouse.

Supporting Survivors

Some friends or family members would like to assist their loved ones, but lack an understanding of sexual assaults and related phenomena. The following advice may benefit those who wish to support their victimized loved one:

Supporters should recognize that the survivor will need to <u>feel safe, be believed, and reassured that the assault was not her fault</u>. If they want to help, family and friends should offer to listen, without judging or questions the victim's actions. Survivors will need to talk about what happened and process or compartmentalize the assault.

Openly discussing such personal information is extremely difficult and draining, supporters should not push it, or pressure the survivor for information. Just listen to what the survivor wants to tell you, and allow the survivor to address the issues she is capable of dealing with at that time, and do not try to rush her recovery.

Supporters should simply try to understand her feelings, and offer her a safe place and attentive ear. They should be there for their loved one, should she feel the need to talk at odd hours, or if she is afraid to be alone. They should encourage the victim to seek professional help, and realize that recovering from a sexual assault will take time, and they will need to be patient.

Once one obstacle is overcome, another one may surface. The survivor is worth the supporter's patience and deserves to feel better and get assistance in processing the trauma she has experienced. Don't try to rush things or *'make it go away'* or *'be all better.'* Healing is a process that will take time. Supporters should respect the victim's choices regarding whether or not she wishes to prosecute the crime – let her regain some of the control that has been taken away from her.

Supporters should educate themselves on rape myths so as not to compound the situation, and should seek their own counseling in order to deal with their own feelings of anger, injustice, and despair. The survivor will have a hard enough time seeking her own recovery; do not add to her troubles by making her address your issues as well.

If the survivor does not feel that she can talk with you without causing you to break down, then she will need to look elsewhere for support, and you don't want her to miss out on any supportive system available to her. Be on her side. If anyone questions her behavior or her version of the event, be on the survivor's side. She may already be dealing with profound trust issues, be a rock for her.

Recovering from a sexual assault can be a long and painful experience. The survivor you know, is worth it, and deserves to reclaim any level of happiness she can on this earth. Be there for her. Encourage her to get help and utilize the resources available to her.

Spiritual guidance is another area where the survivor may experience some difficultly. Questions such as, *"why did God let this happen to me"*, *"Does God hate me or is he punishing me for something"*,

"God must not exist, otherwise he would have protected me" may arise. The survivor's spiritual and religious health may also be affected by the sexual assault. Aid her or direct her to resources to assist her in answering these very tough questions.

Do not force the survivor to 'forgive' her attacker. Many 'Cultural Christians' have the mistaken and unbiblical belief that if you are a Christian, then you must forgive everyone who wrongs you (or else God would not forgive them). This is incorrect, unbiblical, and maladaptive.

The Bible is very clear about God holding the wicked accountable for their actions. The survivor of a sexual assault is entitled to justice, and should not be forced to remove the consequence of an evildoer's actions out of a failure to understand Biblical principles. To gain a better understanding of the Biblical concept of forgiveness, and when it is appropriate, I suggest reading, *'Hate Evil, Love Good, and Establish Justice; Re-examining Christian Teachings on Forgiveness and Confronting Evil,'* by Daniel Loeb. The book also has an appendix that examines Rape from a Biblical perspective.

It is truly unfortunate, but like many other crimes, the victims of rape may not receive justice while on the earth. Law Enforcement or the Prosecutor's Office may not be able to successfully prosecute the case, but even if they were able to, that does not mean justice has been served. Some acts are so atrocious, that there is no earthly punishment that would suffice. In such cases, it is important to have faith in God, to believe that He is a God of Justice, and to trust that He will hold the evildoers accountable for their deeds.

Nahum 1:3 God hates evil and in no way will He acquit the wicked.

Luke 18:7-8 shall God not avenge His own elect who cry out day and night to Him? [8] I tell you that He will avenge them speedily.

Appendix One

— **Rapist Profiles** —

Stranger Rape: the three major categories of stranger rape include the Blitz Attack, Contact Sexual Assault, and the Home Invasion Sexual Assault.

Blitz Attack: the perpetrator ambushes and brutally assaults the victim with no prior contact. Blitz assaults usually occur at night in a public place.

Contact Sexual Assault: the perpetrator contacts the victim and tries to gain her trust and confidence in order to place her into a position where she can be attacked. Contact rapists select their victims in pubic places and try to lure them into isolated locations where they can successful assault their victims.

Home Invasion Sexual Assault: occurs when a stranger breaks into the victim's home in order to commit the sexual assault, or breaks into the home for other criminal purposes and commits the sexual assault out of opportunity.

The 2000, *'Victim, Incident, and Offender Characteristics,'* published by the National Center for Juvenile Justice (NCJJ), analyzed sexual assault data collected by law enforcement agencies over a five-year period, and the following characteristics were found to be significant among victims of sexual assault:

Offenders: 77% were adults, 23% were under age 18, and 96% of the offenders were male. Approximately 59% were acquaintances of their victims, 27% were family members, and 14% were strangers.

In order to investigate and respond to stranger rapes, forensic psychologists and law enforcement agencies have complied profiles of rapists that they can use as part of their investigations and/or prosecutions of rape cases. Rapists are placed into four categories. Of course, not every rapist is going to fit perfectly into one category, but by studying convicted rapists and through other research, common traits have been identified, allowing rapists to be grouped into these four categories. The profiles provide information that may be useful while investigating a specific kind of attacker or the information may prove useful during their apprehension or interrogation. Profiles of rapists are based on their motive, style of attack, and psychosexual characteristics. The four profiles are: the power-assertive rapist, anger-retaliation rapist, power-reassurance rapist, and the anger-excitation rapist.

– Power Assertive –

Traits: the Power Assertive Rapist is usually athletic and views himself as being 'Macho'. This is the type of rapist who commits date rapes. He usually selects his victim at bars or night clubs, and attempts to isolate his victim. He might offer her a ride home, or use some other form of persuasion to isolate his victim. He looks for opportunities and vulnerabilities. Once his victim is isolate, he will become physically aggressive, and will use whatever amount of force is required to subdue his victim. He may use degrading language, display a weapon, slapping/punching, or the weight of his own body to control his victim. This type of rapist does not intend to kill his victim.

Motivation: the Power Assertive Rapist is insecure, but presents himself as being confident. He wants to posses (not harm) his victim, but he will harm her in order to gain control of her. He feels inadequate around women, and desires to assert himself over them in an effort to confirm his masculinity. He rapes because he believes he is entitled to it.

Method of Attack: he is a persuasion predator who first attempts to con his victim in order to place her into a position of disadvantage, and then he may utilize a violent Blitz attack. He will limit his level of violence to the amount of force required to subdue his victim, which may only amount to verbal threats. He may display a weapon, but this is done mainly to gain cooperation. His goal is to humiliate, not to torture. His manhood is in question, so resistance may cause him to increase the amount of force.

– Power Reassurance –

Traits: the Power Reassurance Rapist lacks self-confidence and social skills. He is unlikely to be involved in a relationship with a woman. He is nonathletic and preselects his victims. He may engage in peeping or stalking prior to an assault, and will often target victims he lives by or works with. He typically breaks into his victim's home early in the morning and surprises her. He uses minimal force, but may threaten his victim with a weapon. He fantasizes that his victim is actually his lover, and may force her to engage in foreplay or act out his fantasies. He is the least violent of the four rapist profiles, and may be dissuaded by screaming, crying, or resistance.

Motivation: He is insecure and feels inadequate around women. He wants to possess his victim, not harm her. The rape is committed in an effort to confirm (reassure) his manhood or restore his self-confidence. He may desire to believe his victim enjoyed it.

Method of Attack: he may begin as a Peeping Tom, but will eventually escalate into a blitz attack. The assault may include verbal threats or displaying a weapon to gain compliance. He may be apologetic or express guilt during or after the assault. He does not desire to cause unnecessary harm.

– Anger Retaliatory –

Traits: the Anger retaliatory rapist possesses anger or hatred for women. He wants to punish, degrade, and/or humiliate them. He often has an explosive temper. His goal is to torture. He looks for opportunities to rape, rather than specific victims. He attacks spontaneously, and is the stereotypical rapist that will leap out from behind the brushes and brutally rape his victims. He is not looking to kill his victims, but he may beat them to near-unconsciousness during the attack.

Motivation: his goal is to torture. His anger may be towards a particular woman, but he directs his rage towards all women, and rapes as an expression of his hatred against all women. His victims are random, and based on vulnerabilities and opportunities.

Method of Attack: he utilizes a Blitz attack that is very brutal – he wants to hurt his victims. He may or may not use a weapon. During the rape he forces sexual acts designed to humiliate his victim. Usually inflicts physical harm prior to sexual harm.

– Anger Excitation –

Traits: the Anger Excitation Rapist is a sadist who derives sexual gratification by inflicting pain on others. He may seem intelligent and charming. He often premeditates and fantasizes about his crimes before attacking. His victims are usually strangers. He may kidnap, blindfold, bind, and gag his victims, and he may rape and torture them over a number of days – often videotaping, photographing, or otherwise documenting the assault. He often kills his victims following or during the extended assault.

Motivation: he receives sexual gratification by causing his victim to suffer. He wishes to inflict physical and psychological pain on his victims, and will eventually kill them.

Method of Approach: he may con or lure his victim into an isolate area, or he may use physical force and/or weapons to gain control. He will humiliate his victim through torture, and cause prolonged pain and suffering over a long period of time.

Appendix Two

— Child Molester Profiles —

Child Molesters are also rapists, but they specifically target children. They too seek out vulnerabilities, and children are some of the most vulnerable members of society. Old Stereotypes of Child Molesters portrayed a dirty old man who hangs around playgrounds offering children candy, but we now know that the majority of Child Molestation case involves a person the child knows – such as a family member, trusted family friend, teacher, sports coach, religious leader, and other trusted person who is given access to a child.

The mental health community has done extensive research on the Child Molesters and has developed profiles of similar offenders. Child Molesters are broken into two categories: Situational Molesters and Preferential Molesters. These two categories are expanded into seven subcategories.

<u>Situational Molester</u>
Regressed
Sexually Indiscriminate
Morally Indiscriminate

Introverted

<u>Preferential Molester</u>
Seductive
Introverted
Sadistic

The Situational Child Molester targets physically or psychologically vulnerable victims, and does not exclusively target children. He exploits opportunities to sexually assault his victims based on their vulnerabilities. This type of offender is the more prevalent of the two categories of Child Molesters, and is more difficult to identify and apprehend. He may exploit a single opportunity, or engage in on-going long-term victimization of a particular child or children. This category of molester is broken down into the followbing four subcategories of behavior: Regressed, Morally Indiscriminate, Sexually Indiscriminate , and Inadequate.

– Regressed Situational Molester –

Traits: the Regressed Situational Molester has a low sense of self-worth, and might begin victimizing children after experiencing a significant stressor in his life (i.e. being laid off from a job). They usually substitute children for their current sexual partner, and often use coercion to gain their victim's compliance. The Regressed Offender targets children in response to a situational occurrence that is usually temporary. He may be in a relationship or even married with a family. He uses children to release the stress he is experiencing in his life, and often molests his own children. Regressed Molesters may have issues with substance abuse, a low self-esteem, and/or poor coping skills.

Motivation: Substitution
Victim Criteria: Availability, Opportunity, Vulnerability
Method of Operation: Coercion

– Morally Indiscriminate Situational Molester –

Traits: the Morally Indiscriminate Situation Molester is primarily motivated by opportunity. He selects his victims based on their vulnerability and availability. His victims could either be strangers or his own children. He will victimize any available person; children are included, but any vulnerable victim will suffice. He engages in behavior that he believes he can get away with, and does not consider the moral implications of his behavior. Victims are selected based on vulnerability and convenience. He is a user of people.

Motivation: Availability, Opportunity, Vulnerability
Victim Criteria: Opportunity, Vulnerability, Children, or Adults
Method of Operation: Lure, Force, or Manipulation

– Sexually Indiscriminate Situational Molester –

Traits: the Sexually Indiscriminate Situation Molester is known for sexually experimenting with children out of sheer boredom. He seeks new and different victims and sexual activities. He does not discriminate between males or females, or the age of his victims. He will abuse anyone available to him at the time, including his own children. This molester experiments sexually, and may engage in bondage, mate-swapping, three partner relationships, etc…

Motivation: Sexual experimentation, Boredom
Victim Criteria: Opportunity
Method of Operation: Lure, Force, or Manipulation

– Inadequate Situation Molester –

Traits: the Inadequate Situation Molester lacks social skills and/or the mental ability to engage in a normal sexual relationship. He may suffer from a variety of psychopathologies, and seeks out children out of insecurity and curiosity. He relates to children better than he does with his own age group. With children he feels safe to explore his fantasies. He may have a mental disorder that makes it difficult for him to distinguish between right and wrong. He is often a loner, incapable of maintaining or establishing personal relations with other adults.

Motivation: Feels safer to experiment with children
Victim Criteria: Strangers or children he knows
Method of Operation: Experiments by holding, fondling, kissing, licking, but not sexual intercourse.

The Preferential Child Molester – also known as a Pedophile – is the other major classification of child molester. This type of Child Molester is sexually attracted to children, and seeks out children as sexual partners. They usually have a large number of victims, who meet specific age and gender requirements, according to the molester's preference – usually within a two year age range. They choose child victims that possess unique psychological and physical characteristics that are associated with the individual pedophiles' fantasies. They are often more organized and methodical than the Situational Molesters. The three subcategories associated with the Preferential Child Molester, they are: Seductive, Introverted, and the Sadistic.

– Seductive Preferential Molester –

Traits: the Seductive Preferential Child Molester seduces his victims. He gives them attention and showers them with gifts and affection. He is usually a master at identifying and manipulating vulnerable children. He grooms his victims and slowly persuades them to engage in sexual acts. He will often attain an authoritative position within his community, and target children who have been previously abused or neglected. He will establish himself as a pillar of society in order to avoid suspicion. He may be grooming or molesting multiple victims during the same time period. After years of abuse – or when the victim grows out of the molester's preferred age group – he will find a way to break contact with the victim, while ensuring the victim's silence (usually through threats, blaming the victims, shame).

Motivation: Sexual attraction to a certain age group
Victim Criteria: Specific age and gender criteria unique to each offender
Method of Operation: Lure, Manipulation, Seduction

– Introverted Preferential Molester –

Traits: the Introverted Preferential Child Molester has a sexual preference for children, but lacks the ability to seduce them. He usually molests children who are very young, and will loiter around places children frequent – such as parks and playgrounds. He has little or no interaction with people his own age, and is usual single. He is often childlike and immature.

Motivation: Sexual attraction to children

Victim Criteria: Children are easier to dominate

Method of Operation: Selects very young children

– Sadistic preferential Molester –

Traits: the Sadistic Preferential Child Molester inflicts physical and psychological pain on children in order to produce his own sexual gratification. He will commonly use a ruse to lure a child, but may also forcibly abduct his victim. He is known for abducting, and will murder his victim in order to avoid detection. He will abduct children from playgrounds, schools, shopping centers, and other public places. He has no love for children, and is only interested in causing them harm and death.

Motivation: Sexual Gratification from torturing others

Victim Criteria: Any vulnerable child

Method of Operation: Ruse, Lure, Forcible Abduction

Child Molesters connect with other likeminded molesters who can help validate/justify their deviant behavior. Organizations such as the

North American Man-Boy Love Association (NAMBLA) and the Danish Pedophile Association provide emotional support to fellow pedophiles, and publish newsletters propagating their beliefs. Child Molesters share child pornography on the internet, share lures and techniques, and justify their fellow molesters' behavior. They are organized and deliberate in their actions.

Bibliography

Bume, Sue, (1998), *'Secret Survivors'*, Ballantine Books

Gardner, Debbie/Mike, (2004) *'Raising Kids Who Can Protect Themselves Paperback'*, McGraw-Hill

Gavin De Becker, *'Protecting the Gift: Keeping children and teenagers safe.'*

Jefferson, Thomas, (1776), *"Declaration of Independents."*

Locke, John, *"Second Treatise of Government."*

Loeb, Daniel, (2009), *'Hands to War: Fighting, Weapons, and Self-Defense for Christian Families'*, Lulu Press

Loeb, Daniel, (2011) *'Hate Evil, Love Good, & Establish Justice: Reexamining Christian Teachings on Forgiveness and Confronting Evil'*, Lulu Press

Scripture taken from the NEW AMERICAN STANDARD BIBLE or the NEW KING JAMES

Strong, Sanford (1996), *'Strong on Defense: survival rules to protect you and your family from crime'*, Pocket Books

- About the Author -

Daniel E. Loeb is a graduate of American Military University, where he earned a Master of Arts degree in Homeland Security, and a Graduate Certificate in Terrorism Studies. He has a Bachelor of Science in Psychology, and an Associate of Allied Science in Airway Science. Master Sergeant Loeb also served as a Sexual Assault Prevention and Response Coordinator Victim's Advocate. He worked as a Law Enforcement Officer at the county level for 10 years. Sergeant Loeb's served two tours in Iraq, and during his latest deployment, he authored and instructed a course on Close Quarters Combat for America's war fighters. He is a Black Belt in Jujitsu, a Defensive Tactics Instructor (for law enforcement), and was a registered coach with USA Boxing. For more information go to **www.dwellwithprudence.com**

Hate Evil, Love Good, & Establish Justice: Reexamining Christian Teachings on Forgiveness and Confronting Evil - takes a deeper look at Christian teachings that may be misconstrued, taken for granted, or only understood superficially. This book seeks to understand what the Bible teaches Christians in regards to their interactions with evil. It endeavors to determine whether or not Christians are obligated to love and forgive everyone, or if certain evildoers and certain sins should not be forgiven. Do parents need to forgive the murderer of their child, or do victims of other violent crimes need forgive their attackers? Does the Bible permit Christians to hate such people? Are there limits to who you are required to forgive? Are there some people that you should not reach out to or pray for? Did Jesus forgive everyone? This book deals with how Christians are to respond to evil. It explores forgivable and unforgivable sins, and includes Bible studies on lying and rape.